M000102414

A NEW PERSPECTIVE ON SELF-ESTEEM

Brain Washed

Transforming Your Self-Image Through the Amazing Love of God

David Nofziger

Copyright © 2019 by David Nofziger. All rights reserved.

All rights reserved. No part of this publication may be reproduced, stored in a retrieval system, or transmitted in any form or by any means – electronic, mechanical, photocopy, recording, scanning, or other – except for brief quotations in critical reviews or articles, without the prior written permission of the author. Contact information for permission requests may be found at HopeAliveCounseling.com.

All Scripture quotations, unless otherwise indicated, are taken from the Holy Bible, New International Reader's Version®, NIrV® Copyright © 1995, 1996, 1998, 2014 by Biblica, Inc.™ Used by permission of Zondervan. All rights reserved worldwide. www.zondervan.com The "NIrV" and "New International Reader's Version" are trademarks registered in the United States Patent and Trademark Office by Biblica, Inc.™

Cover design by Michael T Skoglund
Edited by Deedra Darby Dixon

ISBN-13: 978-1-7945-6096-3

DEDICATION

To Sue, my wife, partner, best friend and the love of my life. We have shared over forty years together, and I love her more today than ever. It was Sue's best friend from high school that paved the way for six years of mission work in England where I began teaching on self-image.

And to my two lovely daughters. We could not be prouder of the godly women they have become, the wonderful sons-in-law they have blessed us with, and, of course, the joy of our golden years, our grandchildren.

A NOTE FROM THE AUTHOR

Dictionary.com defines brainwashing as:

- A method for systematically changing attitudes or altering beliefs, originated in totalitarian countries, especially through the use of torture, drugs, or psychological-stress techniques.
- Any method of controlled systematic indoctrination, especially one based on repetition or confusion.

It is terrible to be brainwashed. To think that an enemy could forcibly cause me to believe something different from what I now believe. To imagine that same enemy being able to get me to behave in a way contrary to my normal behavior. But even more shocking, if that enemy is successful, I end up not only doing what they want me to do, but also doing it with all my heart believing it is the right thing to do. That is the result of a thorough brainwashing. Why can a person be brainwashed in this way? It doesn't make logical sense. But understanding the answer to that question can actually help us discover the secret to being able to change our own lives in a positive, healthy way.

Truth be told, this book is not a spy novel nor a book about brainwashing techniques. It is actually a book about building a healthy self-image. But now that I have your attention, let me explain the reason for the title. Note, the title is <u>Brain Washed</u>, not Brainwashed. Yes, a play on words, but a very important play on words. When we make it two words, we totally change the connotation.

The idea that our brain could be washed (cleansed or renewed) is a very intriguing concept. We have all been hurt, lied to, betrayed, misused, and abused, which has left deep scars that fill us with frustration, bitterness, and emotional pain. Not only that, we have all hurt others, which plagues us with guilt and regret. These experiences produce negative inner beliefs which damage our self-image and rob us of peace, joy, and fullness of life. They negatively affect our health and wellbeing more than anything else. They can fill us with insecurity, fear, frustration, and shame, causing us to feel unloved, worthless, and unacceptable.

What if the brain could be washed in a way that changed these negative beliefs into positive beliefs? You don't think that is possible. Well, if an enemy can change our beliefs in a negative way against our will, why can't we discover how to change our own beliefs in a positive way in order to transform our self-image?

I firmly believe we can, and I am first and foremost speaking from personal experience. My self-image went through a radical transformation in my young adult years, and I came through that period seeing my life changed in wonderful and amazing ways. I went on to earn a Master's Degree in counseling and have been a professional counselor for the past 35 years.

But the most fascinating aspect of the transformation of my self-image is that the change happened through my relationship with God. Coming to deeply know and understand the amazing love of God is the single greatest factor that can transform self-image.

If you are one of the millions of people who suffer from a low self-image, I believe that your self-image can be transformed in a way that radically changes your life for the better!

David Nofziger

CONTENTS

Part I Understanding Self-Image

Part II Understanding Esteem Needs

Part I
Understanding Self-Image

INTRODUCTION TO PART I

I will never forget the first day of a two-year graduate program in Pastoral Psychology and Counseling. One of the classes that day was "Self-Esteem 101" (I can no longer remember the actual name of the course, but this is close enough). The class was being taught by the head of the counseling program, Dr. Richard Dobbins, PhD; Founder of Emerge Ministries in Akron, Ohio.

As he began writing on the large blackboard at the front of the class, he started listing on the left-hand side, five symptoms of a low self-image. As he listed each belief and the symptoms associated with those beliefs, I thought to myself, *"Those all look very familiar."* I wondered, *"Do I have a low self-image?"* To be honest, I had no idea at that point what self-image or self-esteem even meant.

Then, on the right-hand side of the blackboard, he began to list the components of a healthy self-image. At this point, a new thought came: *"Those are the changes God has been making in my life over the past five years."* Radical, wonderful, life-transforming changes. I was very grateful for the changes even though I hadn't fully understood what God had been changing.

On that day and the rest of the semester, I started realizing that God had been changing my self-image. What fascinated me most was that the changes were happening naturally through my growing relationship with Him. Plus, those changes were helping me become more like Jesus Christ. My changing self-image was enabling me to be *"conformed to the image of His Son"* as described in Romans 8:29. This revelation gave me a keen interest in understanding self-image, and over the past 35 years as a counselor, I have enjoyed helping others develop a healthier self-image through an ever-deepening intimacy with God. I trust you will enjoy going on this journey with me; perhaps your self-image will be radically changed in a positive way as well!

CHAPTER 1

MY STORY

To help you understand what had been happening in my life during the five years prior to beginning my counseling training, I have to go back much further and tell you a little of my story.

I grew up several miles outside of a small town in Northwest Ohio with three siblings: a sister eleven years older, a brother seven years older, and a brother three and a half years younger. My mother worked full time and was the financial support for the family because my father had bipolar disorder, a mental illness that can cause extreme mood swings from mania to depression. This made it difficult for him to hold down consistent employment and created some interesting family dynamics as I was growing up. My father's mental illness gave me an interest in mental health and was probably an integral part of my deciding to enter the field of psychology and counseling.

The most significant aspects of my story involve my spiritual development. My family attended church regularly. When I was eight years old, a special guest speaker gave an invitation to receive Christ at the end of his message. During the invitation, my father leaned down and asked, "Would you like to go forward and receive Christ?" I felt a strong connection with my father as well as a strange stirring inside, so I nodded my head in affirmation, and we went forward together. I remember kneeling at the front of the church with our pastor and asking Christ to forgive my sins and come into my life as my Lord and Savior, often referred to as a prayer of salvation. Being only a few short years out of the Santa Claus stage, it was easy to believe that God was real, I could ask Him into my life, and He would forgive me and accept me as one of His children. I believed that I was now part of the Family of God and headed to Heaven at the end of my time here on earth.

The next significant event affecting my spiritual walk with God came when I was thirteen. I was now well out of the Santa Claus years and remember wondering one day at school, *"Is God really real, or is He just someone adults tell us about to keep us in line?"* (I sometimes find my memories fascinating.) Needless to say, that was a critical time for me spiritually. Fortunately, God allowed me to experience something that ended those doubts forever. Once again, it involved my father.

Besides being bipolar, my father developed Multiple Sclerosis when I was ten. It took almost three years for the medical community to make a diagnosis, and during those three years, he was in and out of numerous hospitals and involved in all kinds of testing. It seemed to me that each time he came home from the hospital his symptoms were worse.

Finally, after three years, they made the diagnosis, and this time he came home from the hospital unable to walk. We obtained a hospital bed with a pull-up bar to help him exercise. Since my mother was working full time, and I was the oldest child at home, I was given the job of being his caregiver. I slept on a sofa in his bedroom as I had to be on call during the night in case the bedpan was needed. Other responsibilities included emptying his bladder bag, giving him sponge baths, and physical therapy three times per day to keep his muscles from deteriorating much further. When my mother was working, I also prepared meals (with some preparatory help of course). You might think that was a lot of responsibility for a thirteen-year-old boy, but I believe it helped me mature and become a fairly responsible person, for which I am grateful.

One of the symptoms he experienced was muscle spasms in his legs. It seemed to happen only once a day, when he and I were going to sleep. It would last for about five minutes, cause his whole bed to shake, and occur every night. He was not experiencing pain, just uncontrollable spasms, but it was emotionally painful for me as I lay there each night trying to go to sleep and listening to his bed shake. I will add at this point that these spasms started several months after I had my "thoughts" about the reality of God.

One night, as his bed was shaking and I was lying there, I clearly remember silently crying out to God and saying, "Please God, take that away and never let it come back." The next night, it didn't happen. In fact, it never occurred again. After that, I had no more doubts. God was definitely real as there was no other rational way to explain what had happened. No one knew of my nighttime plea, only God, and He had answered the simple prayer of a young teenager.

The next significant period came the summer after my junior year of high school. Let me tell you a bit about myself at this age. I disliked myself in a variety of ways: My physical appearance; the fact that I was shy, a loner, and very quiet; and the belief that others would not want to be my friend. All common symptoms of a low self-image.

In contrast, I did love sports, especially basketball and baseball, which were the two main sports in my little town. There were 37 students in my class, so you can see it was quite small. Basketball was my favorite sport, and I spent many hours practicing as we had to log one hundred hours over the summer in order to qualify for the varsity team. Needless to say, we often had some good teams.

To say I was a quiet teenager is an understatement. To be honest, I barely talked at all. As a freshman, I had a speech class in which I had to give one five-minute speech. I dreaded every minute and thought I was going to die of embarrassment! One thing I definitely knew: public speaking was not in my future.

I enjoyed singing but was much too shy to sing in public. Halfway through my junior year, the choir director informed me that I had a nice bass tone and talked me into singing a solo at a community concert. Now it was known I could sing.

At the end of my junior year, one of my classmates informed me that a youth choir was starting that summer in her church. They would be singing in different churches, and she asked if I would like to join. I agreed to join the choir, which had about thirty members, and had a wonderful experience. For the first time in my life, I felt as if I was doing something useful for the kingdom of God. Before that time, I knew that I loved God and was grateful for his salvation, but felt somewhat useless as a Christian (another common symptom of a low self-image). This increased sense of usefulness was giving me a joy I had previously not known.

Then I started having thoughts that God was calling me into the ministry. In my mind, that meant being a preacher which also meant being a public speaker! I knew those thoughts could not be from God because He knew me better than that. I simply tried to put that out of my mind, but the thoughts persisted. Were they actually coming from God? I then began explaining to God why I could not be a preacher. Of course, the number one reason was that I could not speak in public, although I had some other good excuses as well – I was too shy, didn't relate to people well, etc. I felt like Moses trying to explain to God why he could not go confront Pharaoh. His number one excuse was that he stuttered. Well, my excuses didn't work either. The thoughts still persisted, so I started running from God. Let me explain.

Toward the end of that summer, as I was experiencing this wonderful joy and thinking that God might be calling me into the ministry, I thought about going to a Christian college. That way, just in case it was God, I would be heading in the right direction. It felt like a wise thing to do at the time since the thoughts were not going away.

As my senior year began, reality started hitting me in the face. I always knew I would be funding my own college education, so during most of my teenage years, I was planning on following in my older brother's footsteps. He had gone to General Motors Institute (GMI), a program in which you went to school for six weeks and worked in a GM plant for six weeks. The six weeks of work paid for the school tuition and living expenses. After graduating with a General Motors Engineering Degree, most students were able to eventually obtain a job as a GM executive, a nice career choice. I had been taking all the math and science I could in high school, and those subjects came easy for me.

As I looked at the prices of private Christian colleges, they seemed totally unaffordable, so I started considering GMI once again. I even went to the nearest GM plant to obtain an application to GMI. As you can see, I was running in the opposite direction. All the joy I had experienced that summer was gone, and I was becoming anxious and depressed.

Early in November, I reached a low point. I remarked to a classmate after basketball practice, "I'm really depressed and don't know what's wrong." (You know it had to be bad if I opened up to someone, I was much too shy to do that.) He simply replied, "Oh, you just need a girlfriend." We both laughed, but I was not laughing on the inside. To make things worse, that night I began filling out the application to GMI. Halfway through, I was feeling very anxious. I stood up and my hand was shaking, which really scared me.

9

I decided to take a bath, hoping to relax. Lying in the tub, I felt God say once again, "Will you follow my call?" I was now through running. I simply responded, "If that is what you want me to do, I will follow, but you are going to have to make a lot of changes in my life!" In an instant, the anxiety was gone, and peace flowed through my body. All the joy I had known that summer came flooding back.

That was the beginning of an amazing journey that has not ended. I could write a book about all the changes that happened during the rest of my senior year, my four years in a wonderful Christian college, and then three years of seminary. I actually did become quite an accomplished public speaker as I was preparing to be a pastor, but the call had actually been for pastoral counseling. It was in the process of following God step-by-step that the call was clarified, and I have deeply enjoyed being a counselor and could not imagine doing anything else with my life.

THE DEVELOPMENT OF THIS BOOK

There I was, on my first day of graduate training to become a counselor. As the instructor was writing on the blackboard, God slowly revealed something amazing. All the wonderful changes He had made in my life after I yielded to His call mainly involved transforming my self-image.

I learned a great deal during that initial class, but I would like to share two lessons in particular. The first is very crucial: My self-image is NOT WHO I AM, BUT RATHER SUBCONSCIOUS BELIEFS ABOUT WHO I AM. Most of us have nebulous opinions about ourselves and assume, *"It is just who I am,"* convincing ourselves by early adulthood that we cannot change. The understanding that my self-image is beliefs rather than fact is vital to discovering that we can change and grow as adults.

The second lesson came from Psychological studies. Some studies were reporting that 95 percent of the self-image is formed by the age of 5. The beliefs we form in those early years tend to stick, and we grow up holding on to those beliefs making them come true. If the beliefs are good and positive, we may be quite productive in life; however, if they are negative or dysfunctional, they can greatly inhibit our growth and wellbeing. Think about that for a minute. How many of you were mature and objective enough at the age of five to form healthy beliefs about yourself? I know I wasn't!

After graduating from seminary, my wife and I left for England. We had accepted a call to serve as assistant pastor at a church pastored by some long-time friends. We served in that role for almost six years, during which time both of our daughters were born.

My main responsibilities were pastoral counseling and specialized teaching programs. As you might guess, one of those programs was on self-esteem. I primarily utilized the materials from that graduate class on self-esteem. The structure of the class was similar to Part II of this book. I would start by discussing the five beliefs and corresponding symptoms of a low self-image (the same five areas that were on the left-hand side of the blackboard that first day of class). We would then examine the beliefs and components of a healthy self-image. The final step involved learning how to change an unhealthy belief into a healthier belief by seeing ourselves as God sees us. We will be discussing this in great detail in Part II.

The classes were going well, but then one family, leaders in the church, began to criticize the teaching on 'self-esteem.' They spoke with the senior pastor, and then made an appointment to talk with me. I was informed that teaching on self-esteem was not biblical, was a source of arrogance and pride, and I should cease teaching on that subject immediately.

11

Now I must add that the family had never attended any of my classes.

Rather than react, I began to gently probe so I could understand why they felt this way. (I must confess, I had to utilize all my counseling skills to manage that one.) They stated that self-esteem teaching was meant to build up the self, and the Bible says that we are to die to self and walk in humility and love for others, not love for self. They went on to mention that they knew some people who had attended self-esteem workshops and had noticeably become prouder and more arrogant.

That helped me understand why they felt it was unbiblical, and I agreed with them in some respects. During the late 1970s and into the decade of the '80s, self-esteem workshops had become quite popular in the United States, and from what they were saying, the same was true in England as well. Most of these workshops focused on feeling better about yourself. You were taught to like how you look, feel positive about your skills, talents, and intellect, see yourself as important and valuable, etc.

Such workshops were so common that the popular television comedy show *Saturday Night Live* was doing frequent satirical skits in the early 1980's which usually involved one of the cast members who was purposely given thick glasses and straggly hair looking in the mirror and arrogantly saying to himself variations of the following statements: "I am handsome and strong, I like myself, I am talented and important, and by golly, I'm just a really nice guy!" The skits were hilarious, but unfortunately, they were similar to what was being taught in the actual workshops. The best satirical humor is just a slight exaggeration of the truth. If the self is built up apart from God, it can lead to arrogance and unhealthy pride.

But I was very aware that the changes God had made in my life had not caused me to become more arrogant. On the contrary, it had actually built a deeper humility. Rather than feeling better about how I looked or how talented or good I was, something was being transformed on the inside. I was feeling deeply loved by God, liking myself better, and caring more deeply for others as well. Then as I looked at the five key components of a healthy self-image which I was teaching, I noticed that none of them involved the outward man, but rather the inward.

With that understanding, I began developing a way to communicate the difference. I separated what I called "ego needs" from "esteem needs" and began adding that to my teaching on self-esteem which I now referred to as, "Building a Christ-Centered Self-Image" (no longer using the phrase self-esteem). I doubt I ever convinced that particular family that what I was teaching was biblical since they never attended any of the classes (fortunately, the senior pastor allowed me to continue to teach on self-image), but I was grateful for the challenge they gave me, as I think it has enhanced and clarified what I teach. This will be explained more fully in Chapter 3, *Ego vs. Esteem Needs*.

After returning from England at the close of 1988, I was able to obtain a professional pastoral counseling position with Hope Alive Counseling Services, an agency which started in 1984. As I began counseling full-time, I realized that many people suffer from a low self-image. Therefore, it was natural for me to continue teaching on self-image.

Then in 1992, I was given a model for the mind which expanded perfectly on the idea that the self-image is subconscious beliefs, many of which are formed in early childhood. This model gave me added clarity on how to empower the conscious mind to change unhealthy subconscious beliefs. I began to utilize it as the psychological foundation as I taught on self-image. We will be fully developing this model in the next chapter.

The feedback I received from clients as I taught on self-image helped me develop a 5 hour workshop in the mid-90s entitled, *The Image of Christ: Building a Christ-Centered Self-Image*. After continuing to teach these principles for over three decades, I have decided to put them into written form to share with a larger audience.

After reading a draft copy of this book, my younger daughter gave me some very helpful feedback. She suggested the thirty day devotional that is at the back of the book. It was an excellent idea to help the reader get into the habit of a consistent devotional time while focusing on key biblical truths which can help meet the needs of the esteem. She also gave me some suggestions for catchy titles. When I saw *Brain Washed, Transforming Your Self-Image through the Amazing Love of God*, I fell in love with the idea immediately.

My prayer is that the truths in this book will help transform your life as it has mine.

CHAPTER 2

A MODEL FOR THE MIND

THE CONSCIOUS AND THE SUBCONSCIOUS

I first heard this model in its basic form in 1992. I was involved with another agency that had come across a program which provided small group interaction and training for those who had been involved in domestic violence incidences. The program was called "Learning to Live, Learning to Love" by Paul Hegstrom. The model was presented in one of his video messages called, "The Power of the Subconscious." I found the model very helpful and saw how it applied to the changes God had been making in my life. Therefore, I began to develop it further and integrate it into what I had already been teaching about the self-image. Of course, the mind is much more complex than any model, but a model can help us gain understanding and insight which in turn can help improve our behavior. It is a way to simplify the complex. This model involves developing an understanding of the subconscious mind, but it is very different from Freud's model. In this model, repressed memories are not nearly as important as the beliefs that have developed because of one's experiences.

The subconscious receives experiences and perceptions and generalizes them into beliefs. Many core beliefs stem from childhood. These beliefs tend to control my behavior, reactions, thoughts, and feelings because whatever my subconscious believes is true for me and comprises my comfort zone. If I have behaviors, thoughts, or experiences which differ from what I believe, I will tend to feel uncomfortable, tense, or even anxious.

UNDERSTANDING THE SUBCONSCIOUS MIND

Now a crucial aspect of this model is the understanding that the subconscious functions at about the level of a five-year-old child. Think of it as a more primitive part of the brain. Like an animal, it reacts to its surroundings based on experiences, i.e., a dog who is mistreated will become very mistrusting while a dog treated well will become very loving. The dog's experiences create beliefs about its world.

So let's examine the thinking of a five-year-old. A young child does not think rationally or logically. He has no problem believing that Santa can come down the chimney, even though that is impossible. Likewise, the subconscious is capable of believing anything at any age. The belief does not have to be based on rational thinking, logic, or reality. For example, I can be an adult and believe I am overweight even though I am not. I will think I am fat and that other people see me as fat, even though most everyone would say I am quite slim. Or, I could believe that only bad things happen to me, even though I experience both good and bad. My subconscious will accept the bad and dismiss the good. Does that make sense? I have often seen both of these examples in my counseling practice.

The subconscious does not think abstractly; like a child, it thinks very concretely. Everything is black or white, good or bad, right or wrong. There are no gray areas with the subconscious. Plus, whatever the subconscious believes is true or right for me. For example, early in my counseling career, I was surprised by how many couples would fight over how to fold towels, which seemed somewhat amusing to me but didn't make much sense.

Do you think there is a right way to fold towels? Do you feel uncomfortable if a towel is folded differently? If you are honest, you will probably say, "Yes." Sorry to inform you, there is no right or wrong way to fold a towel; there are simply different ways of folding towels. But this is an abstract concept that the subconscious cannot understand. For the subconscious, the way you fold towels is right (which was probably the way your mother folded towels). If someone folds a towel differently, you feel uncomfortable and tense and want it to be folded right. If a married couple folds towels differently, each thinks the other is folding it wrong and argue about who is right.

As I explain this concept to clients, their initial reaction is: *"That's why **they** always have to be right!"* We are not as aware that I always have to be right as well. I simply think, *"I am right. Right?"* But others have to be right even though I think they are wrong (I trust you are getting my point).

My subconscious beliefs affect every area of my life: I have beliefs about myself, relationships, religion, politics, people, and the world to name only a few. All my habits are driven by subconscious beliefs. These beliefs are on a continuum of strength. A belief can be mild, moderate, strong, or anywhere in between. For example, I could have a very mild belief about the right way to fold a towel, and it may not affect me much if my spouse folds it differently. But if I have a strong belief about the right way to fold a towel, I will feel tense, even angry, if my spouse folds it differently.

During the first five years of my life, I am functioning at a subconscious level only. Whatever I am experiencing is being

17

generalized into beliefs. Thus, beliefs can form fairly quickly. During our counseling training, one of my classmates shared the following example after we had learned about the importance of the father in the development of a child's self-image. The example involved an event that had recently occurred with his five-year-old daughter.

First, he let us know that his daughter was *as skinny as a rail*. One night she had an exceptionally good appetite and had eaten a big meal. As she was working on her piece of pie, he said, "You're eating a lot, you'd better watch it, or you're going to get fat." Then he smiled and chuckled because he was just teasing and making fun of how thin she was. Later that night, they were playing on the floor. He was on his back, and at one point, she was on her back, lying crossways over his stomach causing her stomach to be rounded and her shirt hiked up. He couldn't resist! After poking her on her bare tummy he said, "Look at that round tummy, you're getting fat." Again, he laughed as he was just teasing. The next day, he noticed that she was picking at her food and not really eating, so he asked, "What's the matter, why aren't you eating? Don't you feel well?" She lowered her fork and her head and sadly replied, "I'm getting too fat." The power of his words on her hit him like a rock. She did not understand teasing; she just knew that her father said that she was getting fat and she believed him. Now, he could correct that very quickly, but when a child is consistently hearing negative things about himself from his parents, he will believe them, even if it is far from true. It will shape what he believes about himself.

Another good example that shows how subconscious childhood memories can negatively affect our self-image as adults comes from my time in England. Jane (not her real name) was thirty when she first came to my office. We walked through her history in the first session. She had four older siblings. The first four were fairly close in age, and she came along ten years later. We had been meeting for about one month when, all of a sudden as we were discussing some of her issues, she burst out in tears and said, "I'm a mistake! It's true, everything I do is a mistake. I shouldn't even be here. My life is awful." The tears were flowing freely, and I could tell she had never shared these feelings with anyone else up to this point.

It did not take a trained psychoanalyst to figure out what she was communicating. Her social history had given me everything I needed to know to make an educated assumption as to what she was saying. What do adults often call an unplanned pregnancy? Yes, I can hear you saying it, "a mistake." That is simply an adult way of communicating. I could just picture little Jane, maybe around four or five years old, sitting on the floor playing with her dolls while mom and a friend, perhaps a neighbor lady, were sitting on the couch chatting away. During the conversation, the subject of Jane's birth is raised and mother politely smiles and says, "Oh yes, Jane was a mistake." Her neighbor knowingly smiles back and understands that Jane wasn't planned but is a precious addition to the family none-the-less, and nothing more is said.

They were not thinking about little Jane being aware of the conversation as she quietly played with her dolls. On that day, Jane learned that she was a mistake. She didn't know exactly what that meant, but her little mind had already learned that a mistake is something that is bad. It started to shape how she saw herself. She started to believe that she was a mistake, and whenever she made a mistake (which is quite often for all of us), it simply confirmed what she believed to be true about herself. When she did something good, her subconscious ignored it or considered it a fluke, but when she made a mistake or did something wrong, her subconscious readily received it because she was a mistake. As she grew older, she learned that a mistake was an unplanned pregnancy. Her low self-image interpreted that as an unwanted pregnancy. She was unwanted and not even supposed to be alive because she was a mistake!

19

Fortunately, this story had a good ending. One of the techniques I used early on in counseling was a method Dr. Richard Dobbins, head of the graduate counseling program I attended, described as "Praying through Painful Memories." First, you communicate the painful memory that has been locked in your subconscious, perhaps for many years. Then you allow the painful emotions to begin to flow as you grieve to God and pour out your heart and feelings to Him. When the tears finally subside, open your heart to God and allow Him to minister to you. It might be a still, small voice whispering words of encouragement or healing. It may be a scene or picture that comes to mind that gives you a healing perspective. It may simply be a sense of His presence and love which covers that painful memory and brings peace.

Jane cried for quite a long time as the depth of that emotional pain was finally released. As the tears began to subside, I encouraged her to take that feeling of being a mistake and see what God had to say about it. As we waited before the Lord in prayer, all of a sudden, she began to laugh. I looked up and asked her what happened. She smiled, "God said, 'I don't make mistakes. Before you were in the womb, I knew you and had a plan for your life.' I think that is in the Bible isn't it?" Of course, she was right, and I quickly got out my Bible Concordance and found the verse in Jeremiah 1:5, *"Before I formed you in the womb I knew you, before you were born I set you apart; I appointed you as a prophet to the nations."*

She had a whole new perspective and could begin to tell herself that she was not a mistake because God loved her and had a wonderful plan for her life long before she was ever conceived. Now, she simply needed to allow God to continue to show her who she was in His eyes. God's amazing love can definitely help transform our self-image.

UNDERSTANDING THE CONSCIOUS MIND

From the ages of five to thirteen, the conscious mind begins to develop. This is the part of the brain that thinks rationally and logically and can understand abstract concepts and gray areas. This part of the brain helps us grow out of the Santa Claus years. We might think of the subconscious as a more primitive part of the brain and the conscious as a more advanced part of the brain. This part of the brain gives us advanced reasoning and makes us different from animals. During this same time, the defenses begin to develop. In this model, the defenses have one main purpose, to protect the vulnerable subconscious. As teenagers, we tend to protect childhood beliefs and reject concepts that differ from these beliefs. If those beliefs are healthy, they help us to stay healthy, but if they are dysfunctional, they can cause us to stay dysfunctional. Early beliefs can stick with us right through adulthood.

For example, two thirteen-year-old boys, Joe and John, are in the same junior high class at school. Joe came from a fairly healthy family. In his early years, he experienced love, affection, affirmation, and consistent, fair discipline. His life was safe and good. By the age of five, he has formed some positive beliefs about himself and relationships. Over the next six years, his conscious mind and defenses are developing. His experiences are no longer going directly into the subconscious. Instead, his defenses block them, and his subconscious reacts to the experiences according to its beliefs. Some of his classmates are treating him well. They are friendly, respectful, and affirming. Joe responds well to this behavior; it feels normal, and he plays frequently with these friends. But some of the boys are not as friendly. They tease, bully, disrespect and laugh at him. Joe becomes defensive and thinks to himself, *"What is wrong with those boys? Why do they behave that way? It's not normal."* He stays away from them and sticks

21

with his *friends*. The defenses are doing their job in protecting him from that negative behavior.

On the other hand, John has come from a more dysfunctional family. In his early years, he experienced very little love or affirmation. He often received messages such as, "You are a bad boy. You're stupid and won't amount to anything." He was disciplined inconsistently. Life was not very safe, and beliefs were forming about himself and relationships. For him, *abuse was normal*. He is in the same class as Joe but is responding to his classmates quite differently. There are some children who are respectful, friendly, and kind. A part of John, at a conscious level, likes that. But deep down inside, he reacts negatively to that behavior. It does not seem normal, it feels fake. Other classmates are teasing, bullying, and being disrespectful. He is more comfortable with this behavior as it feels normal. Friendships are built with these boys, and he behaves in the same way. He gets labeled as a "bad boy" by teachers and other classmates, and the cycle of his childhood is repeated. This can continue right into adulthood and never change.

This also helps us understand why psychologists say that 95 percent of our self-image is formed by the age of 5. The beliefs formed in those early years start to be protected by our defenses, and we tend to keep those same beliefs right into adulthood.

EMPOWERING THE CONSCIOUS MIND

But this is where the most important part of this model comes into action. *I must discover how to empower the conscious mind so that I can change unhealthy subconscious beliefs*. This model declares that *any* belief can change at any age, but it is not easy to change a subconscious belief. What makes it hard? The defenses and the strength of the belief. The defenses are constantly blocking experiences that are different than the subconscious belief, and the stronger the belief, the more I will tend to resist change.

Two key ingredients are needed to change a subconscious belief: insight and consistent proactive changes. In other words, I have to gain insight into the unhealthy belief (a conscious process) and form behavior and thinking goals which are healthier. Then I have to practice behaving and thinking consistently according to those new goals. After a period of time, the subconscious belief begins to adapt and move until it matches my consistent proactive behavior and thinking. This is similar to how we train animals. We positively reinforce behaviors that we have them repeat over and over with verbal cues until they perform immediately upon command. A belief has formed that is now habitually driven by the verbal cue. As we gain insight and strengthen our conscious mind, we can *train* ourselves.

I previously mentioned that every habit is directed by a subconscious belief. If you have ever changed a habit, you have a little insight into how to change a subconscious belief. First, you set a goal to behave differently because you didn't like the old habit. If you succeeded in consistently practicing the new behavior long enough, you discovered that, eventually, the behavior became a new habit.

Anything that is a habit or subconscious belief, I will do without thinking (it bypasses conscious thought). Anything that is not a habit or subconscious belief, I will not do without consciously thinking. To change a habit, I have to consciously choose to do the new behavior. Therefore, I need something to regularly remind myself to do the new behavior over and over again.

The subconscious desires to drive my **behavior, thoughts, reactions,** and **feelings**. When it succeeds, I am in my comfort zone. If I choose to behave differently, I feel some discomfort and tension. The subconscious keeps trying to pull me back to the old behavior. With no insight, I tend to concede and fall back into my comfort zone.

Key goals have to involve **behavior** and **thoughts**. I can consciously choose to behave any way I want, but if I behave in a way that is different from what my subconscious believes, I will feel tense, uncomfortable, anxious, and perhaps even angry. I can calm that reaction somewhat by speaking to myself, but I have to speak to myself the way I would speak to a five-year-old. For example, I can say to my subconscious in a very calm, safe way something like this: "I know you are uncomfortable, but it's OK. This is a good thing and I am going to continue to behave in this way." When I do this, I will often find myself relaxing a little. Because I speak in a safe way, the message is able to penetrate the defenses, and the subconscious hears it even though right now it does not fully believe it.

I can also choose my **thoughts**. This is more difficult than choosing my behavior, but is still possible, especially with practice. I set thought goals and remind myself to think those thoughts on a regular basis. For example, in marriage counseling, I will often teach my clients to regularly think this thought concerning their spouse: *This is the most important person in my life. Have I shown that consistently in my behavior today?"* My subconscious experiences this thought every time I think it. The thought also reminds me how to behave, a double bonus. As I think this thought consistently and choose to behave accordingly, my subconscious will gradually build a belief that my spouse is highly valued, and my behavior will begin to naturally match that belief. You might think, "I already highly value my spouse, why do I need to think this thought?" If that is true, wonderful, but I will simply ask, "Does your behavior (not your intentions) consistently prove you highly value your spouse?" Make sure you get some feedback from your spouse as well. If not, your subconscious may not firmly believe that your spouse is the most important person in your life and may possibly be driving some unhealthy behavior.

I can choose my **reactions**, but that is even harder. Experiences happen, and the subconscious reacts, bypassing conscious thought. But with insight and practice, I can start to intercept those reactions and consciously choose to respond proactively. This takes time, and I have to be patient with myself.

Lastly, it is very difficult to choose my **feelings** because many of my feelings are rooted deep in the subconscious and will simply reflect what the subconscious is believing. What I discover through this model is that I can guide my feelings through proactive behaviors and thoughts. As the belief changes, the feelings begin to change. I can use my feelings to gauge how I am doing in changing the belief.

The fact that any belief can be changed is shown in a negative sense by the fact that I can be brainwashed. This model helps us understand brainwashing. An enemy will impact me with experiences, words, or concepts repeatedly in different ways. If their messages succeed in changing the beliefs they are targeting, I will not only do what they want me to do, but I will do it with all my heart, believing it is the right thing to do. That is the power of subconscious beliefs.

On the positive side, God desires to *"wash"* my brain by renewing my beliefs through the Bible. The Apostle Paul describes this perfectly in Romans 12:2, *"Do not conform to the pattern of this world, but be transformed by the renewing of your mind."* He also spoke of cleansing our minds through the washing of the Word (the Bible), *"Cleansing her by the washing with water through the word"* (Ephesians 5:26).

GAINING INSIGHT INTO
SUBCONSCIOUS BELIEFS

Since these beliefs are below the level of my conscious awareness, how do I gain insight into what my subconscious is believing? Reading good books on different growth topics can help with insight. Books can take me beyond my limited experience and help me to consciously understand what healthy thinking and behavior look like. Books can give me new behavior goals as well as new ways of thinking.

Over my many years of counseling, I have had a number of court-ordered domestic violence cases. One of the main goals for domestic incidences is anger management training. Since I had not specialized in anger management training, one of the counseling goals was that these clients had to read six books on anger management. Each week, clients had to come to the session and teach me what they were learning. What amazed me the most was the changes I saw happening in the clients' thinking after about the third or fourth book. They were experiencing insight which was changing how they saw anger in themselves and in others and were starting to manage their own anger more productively. I realized that a key factor was that they were learning similar concepts from different perspectives with each book, and it was gradually making more sense to them. The insights started to change their thinking, which then began to change their behavior and reactions.

We can also gain insight through targeted self-examination. Some of my beliefs are healthy. With these healthy beliefs, I behave well, think well, react well, and have healthy feelings. I feel like a competent adult. I do not have to be that concerned with healthy beliefs unless I desire to strengthen a healthy belief. But we all have beliefs that may be unhealthy, dysfunctional, or even irrational. These beliefs drive unhealthy behavior, reactions, thinking, and feelings. When these beliefs are in action, I often feel like a child and try to hide the resulting behaviors from others (but I rarely succeed because they are subconsciously driven and I behave without thinking). My conscious mind does not like it, but with no insight, I simply shrug and think, *"I guess this is just who I am."* If someone points out the unhealthy behavior, I am uncomfortable and can get very defensive, even angry.

Therefore, my goal is to examine the unhealthy behavior and seek to gain insight into the unhealthy belief instead of simply ignoring the unhealthy behavior. How do I accomplish this? Well, if I knew all of my subconscious beliefs, all my behaviors, reactions, thoughts, and feelings would make sense. Not necessarily rational sense because the beliefs may not be rational, but they will be congruent with the belief. With that knowledge, I can work backward. I can ask myself, *"What might I be believing that would cause me to behave, react, think, or feel this way?"* At first, I may simply be making an educated guess, but the goal is to define what the belief might be. As I keep working at it, I start to gain a better understanding and insight into the belief.

It is similar to putting together a jigsaw puzzle. With no insight, it is like the puzzle has been dumped on the table without a box to see what the picture might be. How do I solve the puzzle? I pick up a piece, examine it, and make a guess. It is blue, maybe it is part of the sky. I set it aside and look for some more blue pieces. As I collect a handful of blue pieces, I look at them more closely and see that some of them start to fit together. I then do that with the rest of the pieces until I have a clear picture of the completed puzzle and everything makes sense. In the same way, I allow myself to look at my unhealthy behaviors, thoughts, reactions, and feelings, and then one-by-one begin to gain insight into the beliefs that may be driving them.

CHANGING UNHEALTHY
SUBCONSCIOUS BELIEFS

When I can define the unhealthy belief, I can then rationally and consciously define a healthier belief and set behavior and thinking goals that line up with that healthy belief. Then I have to remind myself consistently to do the healthy behavior and think the healthy thought. Eventually, the unhealthy belief will shift and become healthier. When the belief changes, I will behave better, react more appropriately, think healthier thoughts, and generally feel better.

Several years ago, I was reading in Proverbs and saw a verse that caught my eye. I began dwelling on it and realized that this verse confirms the model I am describing here in a wonderful way. The verse is Proverbs 3:3, *"Let love and faithfulness never leave you; bind them around your neck, write them on the tablet of your heart."*

The verse points to two qualities that are very important, but if these qualities are not a regular part of our lives, there is a two-step process to incorporate them into our lives. First, I have to *"bind them around my neck."* That means I have to do something to remind myself to be loving and faithful. If I take it literally, I would put on a necklace that says, "Be loving and faithful today." It does not matter how I remind myself, but I must because if it isn't a habit, I will not do it without thinking about it. But here is where it gets exciting. As I choose proactively to be loving and faithful on a regular basis, eventually, I can throw the 'necklace' away, because it will be *"[written] on the tablet of my heart."* My subconscious will believe that I am a loving and faithful person, and I will behave that way without thinking and be uncomfortable and tense if I am unkind or deceitful.

This verse also brings up another important point. There are many important qualities that I need to have in my life, and many issues I need to work on. But unfortunately, I cannot work on them all at once. Working on one or two goals at a time is the best way to change. If I try to do too much, the tension will be so great that I am guaranteed to fail. The perfect example of this is our New Year's resolutions. Most of us have tried annually to make resolutions, and after failing each year we often give up and think, *"I guess I can't change."*

But we often go about it all wrong. First of all, I make too many resolutions. Then I proceed into the new year as if it is a sprint rather than a marathon. For example, I am going to lose weight, so I cut out all fats, carbs, sugars, and almost starve myself. I am going to exercise, so I hit the gym, work up a sweat, and totally exhaust myself. I am going to stop smoking, so I do it cold turkey. Plus, I have a few more goals I am trying to work on. I do all these things at once starting New Year's Day. Several days later, I am starving, sore, craving nicotine, etc. By January seventh, I feel like it has been four months rather than seven days, and each day something inside is begging me to go back to the way things were. It wasn't so bad, right? After about two or three weeks, I finally give up in defeat and tell myself once again, *"I guess I just can't change."*

Now let's try it in a healthier way. I set two goals: I am going to diet and exercise. I set realistic weight loss goals based on my metabolism (some people can lose weight faster than others with the same calorie intake) and find an eating plan that reduces calories while providing good nutrients and proteins to fuel my body. Then I plan my meals, reduce snacks, and seek to eat in a way that I can easily make into a lifelong pattern.

I set exercise goals, starting out slowly and gradually increasing until I reach a realistic program which I can maintain for a lifetime and enjoy. It will still be difficult, but as I encourage myself each day and stay consistent, it will gradually get easier and become a habit. Then I can simply enjoy the results.

Actually, these two goals are vital to a healthy life, although I would like to change the word diet to healthy eating. I say this because we often refer to the word *diet* as some type of weight loss scheme, and there are lots of those available. But the best way to stay healthy and increase your energy is simply to eat healthy foods and to exercise. Plus, meeting these goals is the best way to lose weight.

Allow me to share with you how I worked those two goals into my own life. It is a good example which shows that slow and steady will trump fast and erratic every time. As a senior in high school, I weighed about 185 pounds and was in fairly good shape, being actively involved in two sports all through high school. I also enjoyed eating and liked a variety of foods. I was not in any sports in college so I would increase about ten pounds during the school year, but then I would lose it all during the summers as I worked construction ten hours a day. After college, I got married. My wife was a wonderful cook, and I no longer worked construction. By the time I turned 30, I was about 25 pounds heavier. My weight was still not bad for six-foot-one, so I did not think much of it. However, I was also not exercising.

In the early 1990s, I began waking up with morning back pain. I remember thinking, *"I'm too young for this."* I obtained a gym membership and began focusing on muscle conditioning, especially my abs and back muscles. After about four months, the morning back pain was gone, and by then I had established a fairly good routine of exercising three times per week. During this time, I had a physical, and my physician encouraged me to lose about fifteen pounds to lower my body mass index to around twenty-five. My physician was a firm believer in nutrition and healthy eating, and he made some recommendations on a change of diet. I tried it for a little bit, but change is hard, and I still felt that my weight was fine.

In the mid-1990s, I was going through a stressful period and, as a counselor, knew that aerobic exercise is good for stress. I decided to add jogging to my exercise program. I'll never forget my first go at it. I took off from my home and jogged for about fifteen minutes. I made it back home, flopped on my La-Z-Boy chair and thought I was going to die! It took about ten minutes to slow my heart rate and be able to breathe normally again. Fortunately, I did not give up at that point; I simply changed tactics. The next time I went out, I alternated jogging and walking for twenty minutes. That went pretty well as I was not exhausted this time and felt energized by the workout. I did that for several months before deciding that I would try jogging for fifteen minutes again. Once again, I was not winded and felt energized. I did that for several months and then increased to twenty minutes. Same results. Several months later I moved to twenty-five minutes and finally to thirty minutes. I do a ten-minute mile, so I was now jogging three miles three to four times a week and feeling great!

By 2012 I was still engaged in the same exercise program, and it was now a well-ingrained habit. If I had to miss a workout, I *really* missed it and couldn't wait until the next time. But even then, I had not lost any weight. I still thought I was at a pretty good weight and loved to eat. Exercising basically helped me to maintain rather than continuing to gain weight as I aged.

By this time, my older daughter had become a nurse practitioner and started working for a physician that was focused on wellness and nutrition. She began studying nutrition and functional medicine and was seeing some amazing results in her clients' health and wellbeing. Of course, she enthusiastically shared these results with her parents and started working on changing our diet and adding nutritional supplements.

My wife started changing our menu, and guess what? I started losing weight. Slowly, over the next two years, I lost twenty-five pounds! It really was not that hard. Our daughter mainly encouraged us to eat natural foods: organic meat, fresh fruits and vegetables, healthy nuts, herbs, spices, yogurts, etc. She gave us some good recipes, and the food was delicious. What we had to cut out, as much as possible, was carbs, sugars, and processed foods. As my wife and I worked together, the transition went quite well. Working as a team always helps.

I understand that you may not have a daughter who is an expert on nutrition, but there are many good books on nutrition and healthy eating that can give you all the insight you need to start eating healthy. Good nutrition is the fuel that drives our health.

Now, I am in my mid-sixties and am at about the same weight and level of conditioning as I was when I was a senior in high school. Most importantly, I feel great and have a lot of energy. Plus, the habit is still well ingrained; the subconscious belief is working well!

Remember the children's story of the tortoise and the hare? Slow and steady trumps fast and erratic every time. It does not matter how long it may take to reach a goal, you just have to keep moving forward and never give up. Once you realize that you can change and have the rest of your life to change, you can continue setting more goals year after year. You will discover that you are a growing, changing person, which is very empowering!

CHAPTER 3

WHY IS A LOW SELF-IMAGE SO COMMON?

Now, we are going to take what we have learned about the subconscious and apply it to the question: Why is a low self-image so common? The self-image is comprised of subconscious beliefs about myself. It is quite common for these beliefs to be low or negative because many of the beliefs are formed in early childhood. At that age, I am not mature enough to make sound, objective, rational decisions about who I am. Therefore, these beliefs are based on my experiences and perceptions in those formative years. Below are some common symptoms of a low self-image:

- Disliking myself
- Feeling unattractive
- Feeling that no one would want to be my friend
- Feeling stupid
- Lying to enhance self-importance
- Deflecting compliments
- Accepting criticism is difficult

- Seeing myself as useless or worthless
- Apologizing frequently
- Needing reassurance from others frequently
- Avoiding new tasks or challenges
- Fearing failure
- Feeling unchangeable
- Feeling inferior to others
- Expecting rejection from others
- Feeling shame or guilt frequently
- Being a people pleaser
- Behaving in self-destructive ways
- Feeling self-pity
- Putting myself down frequently
- Being overly harsh on myself
- Forgiving myself is difficult

This is far from an exhaustive list, but it helps as we examine our own thoughts, feelings, behaviors, and reactions. I must admit that I felt many of these symptoms when I was a teenager. You might ask, "What are some factors that help create a low self-image?" Of course, there are many factors, but I will focus on a couple of the most common.

Dysfunctional and abusive families can deeply affect our self-image. Verbal and emotional abuse implant negative messages into the child which are easily believed at a young age. I have had so many clients over the years tell me of the hurtful words and messages they received consistently from those who were supposed to love them the most. Those are the same messages they now tell themselves on a regular basis as adults. The saying, "sticks and stones may break my bones, but words will never hurt me," could not be further from the truth.

Physical abuse is very similar. A young child sees life from an egocentric perspective. An eight-year-old child who is physically struck by an angry parent does not say to himself, *"My dad really has an anger management problem!"* Instead, he says something like this, *"I must be really bad to make daddy so angry at me."* The first thought is much truer than the second, but the child believes the latter. Furthermore, an abusive parent often blames the child, which reinforces what he already believes about himself. I had a forty-year-old client vividly recall an event which happened thirty years prior: "In a moment of rage, my father grabbed me, threw me against the wall, then walked up, stuck his finger in my face and yelled, 'Now look at what you made me do!'" The accusation coming from the father reinforces the child's natural tendency to blame himself which drives the unhealthy belief deep into the subconscious.

Sexual abuse can be very similar as children often blame themselves or see themselves as the cause of the abuse. I have counseled with victims of childhood sexual abuse who had more anger directed toward themselves than their abuser. They could not understand why they allowed the abuse to keep happening. Children are often paralyzed by abuse and have no concept of the power of an adult over a child.

One case, in particular, showed me how powerfully sexual abuse can damage the self-image. I met with her early in my counseling career. She was thirty when I first saw her. I will often walk through a person's history to get to know them better. Early on, she informed me that she was molested by an older brother. As she continued her story, most of it revolved around her boyfriends, and she was rarely without a boyfriend during all of her teen years. With each relationship, she described how she was mistreated and disrespected, and she declared that they all just wanted one thing. By the time she was eighteen, she had experienced two date rapes. As she continued into her twenties, she never married but had numerous relationships with men. Once again, she was mistreated by each one, and her anger was growing as she recalled each relationship. I remember thinking, *"Not all men are like this. Why did she have the misfortune of only meeting this kind of men?"*

When she finished her story, I looked at her and asked, "Haven't you met anyone who treated you with dignity and respect?" She looked me right in the eye and said, "Oh, yes, but I just thought they were stupid." Now, I was trained not to react and was grateful for that training. I simply continued to look her in the eye and asked, "What do you mean stupid?" She replied, "They are just stupid." I asked her the same question again, and she gave the same answer. Then I changed my question slightly, "Why are they stupid?" She thought for a moment and declared, "Well, they are stupid for treating me that way." She was now implying that she did not deserve to be treated with dignity and respect, so I continued, "How do you feel when a man comes up to you at the bar, offers to buy you a drink, begins to flirt with you as well as adding a few sexual innuendoes?" Her eyebrows raised a bit, and she deepened her eye contact. I could see she understood where I was going with my question, but I appreciated her honesty. She simply replied, "I like it." Of course, I was describing a man on the make, someone looking for a one-night stand, the very type of man that would misuse and disrespect her, but she was drawn to this type of man.

We then went on to talk about some of the men she had met who treated her with dignity and respect. She confessed that she felt uncomfortable around them. It didn't feel normal to her, and she was able to discuss the fact that she did not feel she deserved to be treated that way. You can see how abuse of any kind can seriously damage our self-image.

Additionally, overprotective families, sometimes called helicopter parents, can also cause a negative self-image. Now, it is good and natural for parents to protect their children. But the protection can become too severe, especially if it continues into the teenage years when the teen is naturally moving toward independence. The teen can see himself as weak or incapable of dealing with problems because the parent always intervenes. He has very little opportunity to develop coping skills because there is not much he has to cope with. A domesticated animal cannot live in the wild because it has not learned how to survive through difficult experiences. Similarly, if a teenager has been overprotected from difficult life experiences as he moves toward the end of his teen years, he may not be ready for the tough challenges he may face as an adult.

Finally, as we saw in our example of John and Joe, a healthy family can build good subconscious beliefs in a young child that helps protect him in school. But the school years can be very tough with children bullying, teasing, ridiculing, etc. The negative experiences can build unhealthy self-image beliefs even in children coming from the best of families.

These examples help us understand why a low self-image is so common. However, I add a very important word of caution. Do not, I repeat, do not blame your parents for your low self-image. Blame creates bitterness and keeps us from growing. Instead, as you read further, realize that Jesus Christ has provided the means for you to be adopted into another family, the family of God. And when God is our adopted Father, we discover that He is better than the best parent anyone could ever have. You can begin seeing yourself as God sees you, and that can revolutionize your self-image!

Also, parents, do not blame yourself for your child's low self-image. That will help no one. Focus on becoming healthier and improving your own self-image through God's unconditional love. That will help your children more than anything else.

EGO VS. ESTEEM NEEDS

Remember the family in England that challenged me for teaching on self-esteem? They knew people who had attended self-esteem workshops and had become more arrogant as a result. I understood what they were saying but did not believe that was happening in my life as my self-image was changing through a growing intimacy with God.

I was grateful for their challenge and perspective because I realized that there may be other Christians who see self-esteem teaching as contrary to the teachings of the Bible. If that is true for you, I would simply ask you to keep an open mind. What follows may be different from what you might be expecting.

With that said, let me introduce you to the five esteem needs listed on the blackboard that first day of class, which form the foundation for this book.

1. The need to be loved
2. The need to be valued
3. The need to be accepted
4. The need to be attractive
5. The need to change and grow

At first glance, it appears that the first four of these needs all depend on how others relate to me. And sadly, I have very little control over how others see me and relate to me. Plus, when I do feel loved, valued, accepted, or attractive, it is usually because of some outward trait or ability that others can see (i.e., physical attractiveness, intelligence, athletic ability, mechanical ability, success, fame, riches, charisma, etc.).

Since I am not in control of how others see me, most self-esteem teaching focuses on building up the self by changing how I see myself. I am to tell myself that I am attractive, smart, athletic, talented, etc., and that other people should like me. I am to affirm myself, rather than relying on others to build me up. If I tell myself these things enough, hopefully I will come to believe it. That is actually in line with the subconscious model, and apart from God, it is about the best we can do to improve our self-image. But it still feels a little fake, and that is why *Saturday Night Live* had such success in satirizing self-esteem workshops. Plus, it can easily lead to what appears to others as arrogance.

I have come to describe this type of self-esteem teaching as building up the ego or meeting **ego needs**. Ego defined as *the outward self or how others see us*. What I have found over my years as a counselor is that meeting ego needs does not necessarily help us feel secure in the center of our being.

Deep down inside, we simply want to be loved or valued unconditionally, not *because of something* (conditional love). I call these deep inner needs **esteem needs**. Esteem defined as the *intrinsic value and worth that comes from the simple fact that I am a human being created by God.*

Let me give a few examples. As a teenager, I was fairly good at basketball. My little town loved basketball, especially when we were winning. There was a degree of popularity that went along with my athletic ability. But deep inside, a little voice would say, *"They wouldn't like me if I didn't help the team win. No one really wants to be my friend or simply likes me for me."* Athletic ability boosted my ego but did not elevate my esteem.

We often think that people who are attractive, talented, intelligent, successful, etc. should have good self-esteem. But often, that is not the case. Outward positive traits or abilities do not necessarily cause us to feel good inwardly, especially if we have some negative subconscious beliefs.

One area in particular surprised me as a counselor. Over the years, I have counseled some very beautiful women. What shocked me was that a number of them shared with me a similar fear concerning their husbands: "Will he love me when I'm old and gray?" Inside they were insecure. They believed that they were loved because they were young and attractive, which they knew would not last. Sadly, they had bought into one of society's greatest lies: *We are loved because of our physical attractiveness.* We will be debunking that myth when we discuss the need to be attractive in Chapter 10.

Allow me to continue because I really want you to understand this concept. The ego always involves comparison. Building up the self by trying to convince myself that I am loved or valued because of some outward ability or trait will not meet my deepest esteem needs. In fact, when that does happen, I often tend to over-accentuate the ego needs in order to feel better about myself. I need to convince myself that I am more attractive, talented, intelligent, successful, etc. than others in order to feel that I have value. Other people will then see me as arrogant or conceited because I am acting like I am better than them. I do not see myself that way; I am simply trying to feel good about myself.

The best biblical example of this is the Pharisees of the New Testament. They had an ego-based religion. They worked hard to be the rule keepers, memorizing all the Old Testament laws and striving to obey them perfectly. They believed that God loved them because they were so righteous. For them, God was a judge, and love had to be earned. God's love was conditional, just like human love. But since that did not meet their esteem needs, they had to be more righteous than others in order to feel good about themselves or to be reassured that God loved them. Jesus described them as self-righteous. We would call them arrogant or conceited. Let's look at one of Jesus' parables, the story of "The Pharisee and the Tax Collector" found in Luke 18:9-14:

> [9] *To some who were confident of their own righteousness and looked down on everyone else, Jesus told this parable:* [10] *"Two men went up to the temple to pray, one a Pharisee and the other a tax*

collector. ¹¹ The Pharisee stood by himself and prayed: 'God, I thank you that I am not like other people— robbers, evildoers, adulterers—or even like this tax collector. ¹² I fast twice a week and give a tenth of all I get.'

¹³ But the tax collector stood at a distance. He would not even look up to heaven, but beat his breast and said, 'God, have mercy on me, a sinner.'

¹⁴ I tell you that this man, rather than the other, went home justified before God. For all those who exalt themselves will be humbled, and those who humble themselves will be exalted.

The Pharisee was standing, proudly reminding God of all the good things he was doing. He thanked God that he was not like certain people – robbers, evildoers, and adulterers. He was comparing himself to others and wanted God to see the difference. Then he looked over and saw a tax collector kneeling and weeping at the altar. Tax collectors were the scum of the earth. He really felt that God must be smiling upon him today.

When he was around *Fred Pharisee,* he didn't feel quite as good. In fact, he felt a little inferior. After all, no one was as good as *Fred Pharisee.* He was the most righteous of them all, and he reminded everyone of that fact regularly. Today *Fred Pharisee* was not around, but this despised tax collector was.

Conditional love always involves comparison. That is why this Pharisee needed to believe he was better than others in order to feel good about himself.

The tax collector knew he was a bad person. He had been cheating people out of their money (we will explain how they cheated people later as we talk about Zacchaeus). He was crying out to God in repentance for his sin, and he experienced the amazing unconditional love and forgiveness of God. He walked away from the temple that day a changed man, a man

41

whose life had been transformed by the love of God. Through this story in Luke 18, Jesus revealed the unconditional love of God in a powerful way.

The unconditional nature of God's love is the heart of this book. In this world, I will always be loved or valued conditionally. My deepest needs will never be fully met. But the Bible reveals a wonderful truth. God loves, accepts, and values us unconditionally. The Bible says it very simply in I John 1:8, *"God is love."* If I can get that truth into my subconscious, my deepest esteem needs can be met. When I come to believe that truth, deep down inside, I become whole. Unfortunately, it can be hard to get the subconscious to fully believe this important biblical truth.

Fasten your seatbelt! We are going on a journey to discover how we can fully receive these wonderful truths found in the Bible. As we travel forward, we may well discover that instead of becoming like the Pharisees, we start looking more like Jesus Christ.

Part II
Understanding
Esteem Needs

INTRODUCTION TO PART II

Now, we move into the heart of this book. Let me give you a brief introduction to my mentor and the founder of Emerge Ministries, the late Dr. Richard Dobbins, PhD (1928-2014). He had been an ordained minister for 25 years before receiving his doctorate in psychology and becoming a psychologist. His strength was the ability to integrate theology and psychology in dealing with the whole person – spiritually, mentally and emotionally. I learned a great deal from his class on self-esteem, but the reason it resonated so deeply within me was that it confirmed and helped explain the changes that had taken place in my life during my late teens and early twenties. The esteem needs that he presented to us were the key areas of change in my life during those years. I knew something had been transformed in my inner being, and I loved the changes, but now Dr. Dobbins was defining the psychological changes that had brought a spiritual transformation in my life.

The insight I gained helped me understand that God had transformed my self-image, and I deeply desired to help others experience that same transformation. Rather than being unbiblical, I believe this message touches on the very heart of the scriptures, the heart of God. God desires to transform my life in a way that enables me to begin to look more like Christ.

As we shall see, that is exactly what can happen when God is able to help us experience his unconditional love and acceptance at a subconscious level.

Perhaps the Apostle Paul described it best in Romans 12:1-2:

> *Therefore, I urge you, brothers and sisters, in view of God's mercy, to offer your bodies as a living sacrifice, holy and pleasing to God—this is your true and proper worship. Do not conform to the pattern of this world, but be transformed by the renewing of your mind. Then you will be able to test and approve what God's will is—his good, pleasing and perfect will.*

Most of our subconscious self-image beliefs are built upon our experiences in this world (how people treat us). Our mind needs to be transformed and renewed by being able to see ourselves from God's perspective. Then we are able to see and do God's will.

Throughout the rest of this book, we will be looking at five key esteem needs, examining each need using the following layout:

1. The subconscious belief and corresponding symptoms associated with a damaged esteem
2. The subconscious belief needed to meet the esteem need
3. The recognition that no human being can adequately meet this need
4. The deepening of our understanding of God in order to allow Him to meet the esteem need and change the belief

I will at times be referring to the **heart** in the chapters to come. I am not speaking about the physical heart, but rather the mind. This word is often used in the Bible to refer to the mind. But drawing from the model for the mind, I like to think of the subconscious as the heart of the mind. Biblical references, especially those that refer to the emotions or deep inner thoughts or beliefs, support this interpretation. Let me give you a few examples.

For as he thinketh in his heart, so is he
(Proverb 23:7 KJV).

I am quoting the King James Version because I like how it translates this verse. We saw how the subconscious beliefs affect every area of our life – behaviors, thoughts, reactions, and feelings. The self-image beliefs are a major part of who I am.

The heart is deceitful above all things and beyond cure. Who can understand it? (Jeremiah 17:9).

The subconscious can contain unhealthy or even irrational beliefs. That is why it is so hard to understand.

And everyone who was willing and whose heart moved them came and brought an offering to the LORD for the work on the tent of meeting... (Exodus 35:21).

The Israelites were moved emotionally to give donations for the tabernacle. Our deepest feelings often stem from the subconscious.

Love the LORD your God with all your heart and with all your soul and with all your strength (Deuteronomy 6:5).

God desires our love to come from the depth, or the core, of our mind.

For where your treasure is, there your heart will be also (Matthew 6:21).

The subconscious beliefs reveal what is most important to us. Jesus also implied in the context of this verse that we can have some unhealthy values or treasures.

For it is from within, out of a person's heart, that evil thoughts come—sexual immorality, theft, murder, adultery, greed, malice, deceit, lewdness, envy, slander, arrogance and folly (Mark 7:21-22).

Our dysfunctional thoughts and behaviors come from unhealthy subconscious beliefs. The damaged heart needs healing so that we can live productive, healthy lives.

Therefore, when I refer to the heart, simply think subconscious, and we will be on the same page. With that said, we shall begin looking at our greatest esteem need.

CHAPTER 4

NEED NUMBER ONE
THE NEED TO BE LOVED

THE UNHEALTHY BELIEF:
I AM UNLOVABLE

Very few people would think to themselves, *"I am unlovable."* No one is unlovable, so that is an irrational statement. But remember, subconscious beliefs do not have to be rational. As we look at the symptoms of this belief, many of us will have to admit, *"Yes, I do have some of those symptoms."* Also remember, all subconscious beliefs are on a continuum of strength. The belief may be mild, moderate, strong, or anywhere in between. For each person, the symptoms of this belief may differ. The stronger the belief, the more one's life will be affected in a negative way. In fact, if that belief is strong, I may have no problem in regularly thinking that I am unlovable and truly believe that no one could possibly love me.

SYMPTOMS OF THE BELIEF

- Disliking myself. I tend to dislike my appearance, am very aware of my mistakes and flaws, am harder on myself than anyone else, and dismiss my successes.
- Thinking that no one wants to be my friend. (I had those thoughts frequently as a teenager.)
- Mistrusting people who befriend me. I might think to myself, *"What do they want from me? They must have an ulterior motive."* Another common thought is, *"They're just pitying me; they think I need a friend."* My mind cannot simply say, *"This person seems to want to be my friend, isn't that nice. I'll return their friendship."*
- Fearing rejection. Even when someone seems to like me, I am afraid that they will eventually reject me, especially if they get to know me.

    I have had numerous clients talk about doing hurtful things to their friends and not understanding why. Let me suggest a possible reason. When I experience something that differs from my subconscious belief, I feel tense or anxious. I subconsciously push this friend away because I am uncomfortable with him being close. Eventually, he decides that the friendship is too hard and backs away. I begin to breathe again and think, *"I knew they weren't really my friend."* I can relax because the rejection has come, my expectation has been met. I feel awful, but at least my life is back to normal. Psychologists call this a self-fulfilling prophecy. I sabotage the relationship without consciously realizing it.
- Finding it difficult to believe God loves me, even though I see it in the Bible.

    I had one middle-aged woman who had been a Christian for over twenty years say to me, "I can believe God loves everyone else in the world. I can believe He loves the worst prisoner in the worst prison, but I can't believe He loves me." It is easy to see how irrational that statement is, but this is a good illustration of how powerfully the subconscious belief can affect our thinking and feelings.

These are just a few of the common symptoms. As a teenager, I could relate to most of them to some degree. I definitely found it hard to believe that anyone would like me – especially when it came to the opposite sex. The following thought was common, *"All the girls that I like don't like me, and the girls that like me I don't like."* I came to think of this as my fate. I realize now that my self-image was affecting my feelings. When I liked a girl, in my mind, it was because she was attractive, friendly, popular, etc. – all the things I thought I was not. I expected her not to like me. If I did end up spending some time with someone to whom I was attracted, I was often so nervous and uncomfortable that I was not much fun to be around. It was hard to simply be myself.

I understand why I thought girls did not like me, but it was harder to understand why the opposite was also true. Every once in a while, I would hear through the grapevine that someone liked me. I can always remember my initial thought went something like this, *"Well, she's not that attractive,"* or, *"She's not my type."* I would immediately negate the idea of exploring a friendship with her. I am not sure why I felt this way; most likely, I was afraid that if she got to know me, she would not like me, and then I would feel doubly rejected. Now with hindsight and a much healthier self-image, I realize that some of those girls were quite nice!

MY SECOND DATE

Let me tell you about my second date. This reveals the power of the subconscious perfectly. It was the spring of my junior year. I grew up in a rural setting with a number of towns within a fifteen-mile radius, each with their own schools.

Brain Washed

There was a youth center about a mile from my home which was started by several churches in the area and was quite popular. On any given weekend evening there could easily be over a hundred teens there from all of the surrounding towns.

I met a sophomore girl from a nearby town who was very friendly and quite talkative. I was attracted to girls who talked easily because I was so quiet. If I was around a quiet girl, nothing was said, and it was uncomfortable to say the least. I had a friend at the time (I know I told you that no one wanted to be my friend, but even though I felt that way, I did have some friends). Anyway, I happened to remark to him one day that I thought this particular girl that I had met at the youth center was very nice. He had a girlfriend at the time and was planning to take her to his church's youth group spring banquet. He immediately smiled and said, "You are going to ask her to the banquet, and we are going to double date." I said, "No." He said it again. I said no again. He said it again. I don't remember how many times this went on, but I finally decided that he was not going to allow me to refuse. Therefore, I thought to myself, *"She's from another town, she doesn't know me. I'll take a chance."*

I asked her out, and she said, "Yes." Wow, she's pretty and friendly and she said, "Yes." We picked her up that evening and headed to the church which was in another town about ten miles away. She was chatting away the whole time, and that helped me to relax and simply listen (something I was good at). We got to the banquet, had a nice meal, and listened to a guest speaker. As we ate, she continued her friendly banter, and I remember thinking, *"She seems to kind of like me."* It was a nice feeling but surprising as well.

Finally, the banquet was over, and we were back in the car ready to head to her home. I had a belief at that time (I have no idea where it came from, but it was there none-the-less): The guy was *supposed* to put his arm around the girl halfway through the date (which was when you got back into the car to head home). I did that on my first date, and now I was feeling the pressure to do it again. After a few minutes, I finally built up the courage to do what I was *supposed* to do, but as soon as I put my arm around her, she sat up straighter and went quiet.

Our subconscious is always telling us what to think, and in the quiet, I could clearly hear the words, *"She may like me as a friend, but putting my arm around her is boyfriend/girlfriend behavior, and she doesn't like me in that way."* It took about twenty minutes to get back to her home, but it seemed like twenty hours to me! I don't recall either of us saying another word, and each minute the negative thoughts increased. By the time we got back to her home, the subconscious words were very clear, *"She hates my guts and never wants to see me again!"* I got out of the car, let her out, and then got back in, barely saying goodbye. I took a deep breath and ruminated, *"How humiliating. Why did I ever say, 'Yes?' This was a stupid idea."* The whole next year, if I saw her at the youth center, I made sure I avoided her as I *knew* she did not want to talk with me.

This story cannot be concluded without telling you what happened two years later. I had just finished my freshman year at the Christian college I was attending. It had been a wonderful year, and I was growing and maturing in many different ways. I was back at the youth center one evening, and there she was. Immediately I thought, *"I need to apologize to her for the way I treated her on our date. I didn't even walk her to the door!"* (You can see my thinking had changed.) It still took me a little while to work up the courage, but then she was outside standing all by herself, and I knew it was now or never.

I walked up and said, "Hi." She smiled and began chatting away, the same friendly person I had gotten to know two years earlier. She had just graduated from high school and was telling me about her plans for college. I shared with her about my first year at college (I was coming out of my quiet shell at this time). I finally said, "I want to apologize to you for how I treated you on our date." I went on to share some of what I had been thinking and feeling.

Her reply was quite surprising. I will share what she said in three parts as each was somewhat of a shock. "Oh yes, I remember that night well, it was my first date..." (She was attractive and friendly; I would not have guessed it was her first date.) "...When you put your arm around me, I just froze, I wasn't sure how to respond..." (Of course, that made perfect sense, but in the two years prior, the idea that she was nervous never crossed my mind.) "...I kind of liked you and wondered why you never talked to me again, but now I understand." For two years, I had been believing a lie, *"She hates my guts and never wants to see me again."* It was far from the truth, but it became true for me. That is how our subconscious beliefs affect our perceptions. You will remember, I was surprised and pleased when I thought, *"She seems to like me."* It took a great deal for me to have that thought, but it did not take much at all to have the opposite thought. The belief that *I am unlovable* makes it difficult to believe that someone might want to be my friend or actually like me. It is even harder to believe that someone would love me for me, with all my imperfections and flaws. But this is my deepest need, the true esteem need.

THE HEALTHY SUBCONSCIOUS BELIEF:
I AM LOVED UNCONDITIONALLY

The deepest, most important need within all of us is to be loved unconditionally. When I feel loved in this way, my life is full; I feel deep joy and wholeness. That is why I call it an *esteem need.* If I do not feel loved unconditionally, there is a degree of emptiness in my life.

You may have experienced a time, with a boyfriend or girlfriend, when you were convinced that he or she loved you unconditionally. She was absolutely enamored with you, and you felt on top of the world. Life was great! But then, when she started pointing out your flaws, you felt she was trying to change you, and you fell into the depths of despair. Sadly, the truth is that no one in this world is perfect and no one will love you unconditionally.

The best we are going to get in a world filled with imperfect people is healthy conditional love, which I will define shortly. But if this is true, how in the world could I ever have a belief that I am loved unconditionally, especially in my flawed condition?

DEFINING LOVE

One of the problems in our society is that the word "love" has such a broad connotation that it confuses us. Your boyfriend says, "I love you." The next day he is talking about how much he loves his new motorcycle and is saying it with much more enthusiasm than when he said the same thing to you. Then he says, "If you love me, you'll let me." Now you are feeling pressured to do something you're not sure you want to do, all in the name of love. Yes, it is all quite confusing.

Sojourners Magazine had a wonderful article entitled, "Have You Tried the Six Varieties of Love?", written by Roman Krznaric and published on December 12, 2013. In the article, he describes six ancient Greek words for love: *Eros* (sexual passion), *philia* (brotherly love or deep friendship), *ludus* (playful child type of love), *pragma* (mature, persistent or longstanding love such as marriage), *philautia* (love of self) and *agape* (unconditional or perfect love). In ancient Greece, each word had its own connotation and helped to differentiate the types of love that we all experience. Love is much less confusing when we see that there are different types.

We all delight in *ludus,* that friendship defined by young children joyously playing together with no prejudices or judgments. *Pragma* is longstanding or marital love which implies commitment and sticking by each other through the good and difficult times. The traditional marriage vows are pragmatic rather than romantic and are expressions of will or choice rather than feelings. The Bible communicates that it is within this type of love that we are to share the joys of e*ros*.

We might think *agape* is what makes a great marriage, but man is not capable of truly attaining *agape*. *Pragma*, combined with a balanced *philia* is what makes a great marriage. *Philia* also makes good friendships. Let me define healthy conditional love. *Philia* is the give and take of friendship love. Here are some examples. *You be nice to me; I'll be nice to you. You be truthful to me; I'll be truthful to you. You scratch my back; I'll scratch your back. You be mean to me; I'll be mean to you* (this last example is similar to the give and take of *philia*, but is not love).

A good friendship, as well as a good marriage, has a nice balance between giving and receiving. But *philia* by itself tends to be selfish. You notice each give and take statement I mentioned starts with a take. "You be nice to me, and I'll be nice to you." We want to receive first, and then we feel free to give. That feels safer for us.

But when both parties in a relationship are doing that, neither gives as each is waiting to receive. There is no healthy friendship or marriage when selfishness rules. *Philia* has to at least move toward *agape* if it is to be healthy. Jesus Christ discussed this beautifully in Matthew 5:38-48 & 7:12:

> [38] *"You have heard that it was said, 'Eye for eye, and tooth for tooth.' [39] But I tell you, do not resist an evil person. If anyone slaps you on the right cheek, turn to them the other cheek also. [40] And if anyone wants to sue you and take your shirt, hand over your coat as well. [41] If anyone forces you to go one mile, go with them two miles. [42] Give to the one who asks you, and do not turn away from the one who wants to borrow*

from you. [43] *"You have heard that it was said, 'Love your neighbor and hate your enemy.'* [44] *But I tell you, love your enemies and pray for those who persecute you,* [45] *that you may be children of your Father in heaven. He causes his sun to rise on the evil and the good, and sends rain on the righteous and the unrighteous.* [46] *If you love those who love you, what reward will you get? Are not even the tax collectors doing that?* [47] *And if you greet only your own people, what are you doing more than others? Do not even pagans do that?* [48] *Be perfect, therefore, as your heavenly Father is perfect.*

[7:12] *So in everything, do to others what you would have them do to you, for this sums up the Law and the Prophets.*

"An eye for an eye, and a tooth for a tooth" is good *philia* teaching. Every good Jew had read that in the Old Testament and agreed with it. That is justice, right? But then Jesus tells them, *"If anyone slaps you on the right cheek, turn to them the other cheek also."* In other words, if someone is mean to you, be nice to them in return. Wait a minute – that does not sound good to me.

"Love your neighbor and hate your enemy." Once again, good *philia* teaching. We like those Old Testament verses and can relate to them well. But again, Jesus says, *"Love your enemies and pray for those who persecute you."* Now you have gone too far, Jesus. I definitely do not like this teaching.

He went on to say, *"If you love those who love you, what reward will you get? Are not even the tax collectors doing that?"* It is easy to love those who love you; everyone does that. But what happens when *everyone* is waiting for *everyone else* to love them? Nobody experiences love, and it becomes a dog-eat-dog world! Sound familiar?

Someone has to start the giving. Let me rephrase what Jesus is trying to communicate in this passage, "Those who know God's love (*agape*) should start the giving." As a human being, I am incapable of giving unconditionally as that would burn me out and ultimately destroy me. I have to receive love as well. But if I wait to receive first, I may be waiting a long time. Jesus was simply teaching us to take *philia* and move toward *agape*. In other words, give first and trust you will receive. That was the **Golden Rule**, *"Do to others what you would have them to do to you"* (Matthew 7:12). Give first, and there is a good chance you will receive as *philia* takes over naturally. But that is a risk. It is not guaranteed and definitely not safe. We need God's help to accomplish this. Jesus ends the Golden Rule by saying, *"...this sums up the Law and the Prophets."* If you love properly, you will be fulfilling every law in the Bible.

In verse 48 he said, *"Be perfect, therefore, as your heavenly Father is perfect."* He is talking about perfect love, or *agape*. The truth is, God is the only one in the universe capable of perfect love. In fact, that is who He is. *"God is love (agape)"* (I John 1:8). The New Testament writers understood that *agape* described God's love. As God's *agape* fills us, we can move toward *agape*, or perfect love, as we receive His love and then initiate *philia* with others, thus fulfilling the Golden Rule.

PHILAUTIA

Allow me to close this section by talking about the sixth Greek word for love, *philautia* (love of self). The Greeks realized that there were two types of *philautia*. They described the unhealthy type as the person obsessed with himself. We see this as conceit or arrogance. At its worst, it becomes narcissism. In contrast to this, they believed the healthy type enables a person to widen their capacity to love others. They recognized that self-love could be good. I believe that when the ego needs are met, but the esteem needs are not, it leads to the unhealthy version of self-love. When God's unconditional love is filling us, we can begin to love ourselves in a healthy way. When I speak of self-love, the latter is what I mean.

Jesus also referred to this type of love in Mark 12:28-31:

> *28 One of the teachers of the law came and heard them debating. Noticing that Jesus had given them a good answer, he asked him, "Of all the commandments, which is the most important?"*
> *29 "The most important one," answered Jesus, "is this: 'Hear, O Israel: The Lord our God, the Lord is one. 30 Love the Lord your God with all your heart and with all your soul and with all your mind and with all your strength.' 31 The second is this: 'Love your neighbor as yourself.' There is no commandment greater than these."*

I need to come to know the fullness of God's love (*agape*) because then I am able to love others as I love myself. God's love produces healthy self-love which deepens our ability to love others.

NO HUMAN BEING CAN ADEQUATELY MEET THIS NEED

As I mentioned before, in a world made up of imperfect human beings, I will never be loved unconditionally. How in the world can I develop a subconscious belief that I am loved for who I am if no one will ever love me unconditionally?

The answer is God. What we learn from the scriptures is that God is *agape* and desires for us to experience His unconditional *agape* love. Then we can draw from that source to initiate love in human relationships in order to help others see God's love in us. In doing this, we start to take on the image of our heavenly Father or as Jesus said, we start to *"be perfect even as my heavenly Father is perfect."*

As we studied the subconscious, we saw that the conscious mind needs to have a rational reason to change a subconscious belief. It is not healthy to choose to believe something that is not true. Therefore, I need to change the phrasing of the healthy subconscious belief just slightly so it agrees with spiritual truth: I must come to believe deep in my subconscious that **I am loved unconditionally by God**.

CHAPTER 5

I AM LOVED
UNCONDITIONALLY BY GOD

GETTING TO KNOW GOD BETTER AND
ALLOWING HIM TO MEET THIS ESTEEM NEED

We have seen that God is *Agape*. He also sent His only Son, who is the exact representation of God, into this world.

> *The Son is the radiance of God's glory and the exact representation of his being, sustaining all things by his powerful word. After he had provided purification for sins, he sat down at the right hand of the Majesty in heaven* (Hebrews 1:3).

We can study the life of Jesus to get to know God better and strengthen the conscious mind's ability to believe in God's unconditional love (something that we have never experienced in this world). The conscious mind needs this in order to be able to get this truth into the subconscious.

God designed the family to be our first introduction to the possibility of unconditional love. Our parents love us simply because we are their children. But because parents are human, they do not always communicate unconditional love very well. A healthy family may come close, but a dysfunctional family may communicate just the opposite. Most of us experience something between these two extremes. For many of us, the only way we are going to come to know God's unconditional love is by getting to know God through the Bible, especially through the life of Jesus Christ. But the Bible is a big book and can be confusing. Even more frustrating is that we tend to interpret the Bible according to what we already believe about God from early childhood. Dr. Dobbins communicated this in a more scholarly way: "Our philosophy affects our theology more than our theology affects our philosophy."

Allow me to illustrate. I will always remember a young man I counseled in England. He had been raised in the Church of England and for several years had been attending the Independent Christian Church where I was the assistant pastor. We were working through various issues as I met with him, and I often talked about God's love. He would frequently respond by saying, "I see God as an Old Testament God," implying that the God of the Old Testament was different than the God of the New Testament. I understood what he was saying. Most likely, during childhood, long before he had read the Bible, a variety of experiences caused him to develop a negative view of God which led to negative subconscious beliefs. As he read the Old Testament, he was able to find verses that confirmed these beliefs, and his subconscious accepted those portions of scripture. It is not difficult to find Old Testament passages where God appears judgmental, harsh, unfair, and even cruel. As he read the New Testament, it was more difficult to find similar passages, and his subconscious was uncomfortable with the love, compassion, and mercy he was seeing in Christ. Therefore, his subconscious dismissed the New Testament and focused on the Old. He interpreted the Bible according to his childhood beliefs rather than allowing the truth of the Bible to change his childhood beliefs.

In seminary, I had been taught to always interpret the Old Testament in the light of the New. My professors used the following verses to help us understand this important concept:

> *In the past God spoke to our ancestors through the prophets at many times and in various ways, but in these last days he has spoken to us by his Son, whom he appointed heir of all things, and through whom also he made the universe. The Son is the radiance of God's glory and the exact representation of his being sustaining all things by his powerful word. After he had provided purification for sins, he sat down at the right hand of the Majesty in heaven* (Hebrews 1:1-3).

Since Jesus represents God perfectly, He is the clearest picture of who God is. God is no different in the Old Testament, but we need the light of the New Testament to properly interpret the Old. My young friend in England needed to understand that his childhood beliefs about God were inadequate and were keeping him from being able to draw from the rich resources of God's love.

EPHESIANS 3:16-19

Let's look at the New Testament and examine God's *agape* love more deeply. We will start with the Apostle Paul. He was one of those self-righteous Pharisees until his life was radically transformed by the love of Jesus Christ.

> *I pray that out of his glorious riches he may strengthen you with power through his Spirit in your inner being, so that Christ may dwell in your*

hearts through faith. And I pray that you, being rooted and established in love, may have power, together with all the Lord's holy people, to grasp how wide and long and high and deep is the love of Christ, and to know this love that surpasses knowledge—that you may be filled to the measure of all the fullness of God (Ephesians 3:16-19).

The Apostle Paul was praying for this young church in Ephesus, and he wanted them to know what he was praying. First, he prayed that they would understand and experience the power of the Holy Spirit in their lives. When we receive Jesus Christ as our Lord and Savior, the Bible says that the Holy Spirit comes and resides inside us. We actually have God, through His Spirit, living within us, never leaving us and desiring to empower us to live godly lives. That alone is amazing, but the next part of his prayer is even greater.

He prayed that they would experience and understand how *wide and long and high and deep* was Christ's love. Those four words represent every dimension, and each dimension is infinite. He was basically saying that God's love is infinite. What a wonderful way to describe unconditional love. Human love, in contrast, is finite. It is like comparing a grain of sand to the universe. There is no comparison.

He went on to pray that they would come to know this love which surpasses knowledge. It is almost as if he is contradicting himself. They were to know something they could not possibly know. They had never experienced anything that comes close to God's love. What he was doing was setting their imagination free! Imagine the greatest love you can, and then realize you are only scratching the surface of God's *agape* love.

Finally, he said that they were to be rooted and established in God's love. You could also translate it *rooted and grounded*. He was referencing botany, i.e., the strength of a tree is in the depth of its roots. A tree with deep roots will be able to withstand the strongest of winds because it is well-grounded. It will also stay green during a dry season when all the other vegetation is turning brown. It is drawing from a source of water that still exists deeper in the ground.

The *roots* of our life are to sink deep into God's love. In other words, we must get the truth of God's unconditional love into our subconscious. If we succeed, Paul states that we will be filled with the fullness of God, and when we are filled with God, our lives are whole and complete!

You might be thinking, *"I would love to be filled with God's love, but I find it hard to believe God loves me at all. I know all my imperfections and the many bad things I have done and wonder how God could ever love me."* If you feel that way, you are definitely not alone. I have heard similar statements time and time again in the counseling office, so let me try to answer the question, "Why would God love me?"

First, He loves you because, as we have already seen in I John 4:8, *"God is love (agape)."* He cannot help but love you. That is the essence of His nature.

Secondly, I believe God's love, if we can receive it deep in our heart (subconsciously), will change our lives and help us become better people. I also believe that much of our sin and bad deeds grow out of our hurts and unmet needs. I do not say this to justify or excuse our sin, but I do want us to see how God's love might help us overcome sin. Let me give you two examples from the life of Christ to show why I believe this to be true.

THE WOMAN AT THE WELL (JOHN 4:3-19)

³ So he left Judea and went back once more to Galilee.

⁴ Now he had to go through Samaria. ⁵ So he came to a town in Samaria called Sychar, near the plot of ground Jacob had given to his son Joseph. ⁶ Jacob's well was there, and Jesus, tired as he was from the journey, sat down by the well. It was about noon.

⁷ When a Samaritan woman came to draw water, Jesus said to her, "Will you give me a drink?" ⁸ (His disciples had gone into the town to buy food.)

⁹ The Samaritan woman said to him, "You are a Jew and I am a Samaritan woman. How can you ask me for a drink?" (For Jews do not associate with Samaritans)

¹⁰ Jesus answered her, "If you knew the gift of God and who it is that asks you for a drink, you would have asked him and he would have given you living water."

¹¹ "Sir," the woman said, "you have nothing to draw with and the well is deep. Where can you get this living water? ¹² Are you greater than our father Jacob, who gave us the well and drank from it himself, as did also his sons and his livestock?"

¹³ Jesus answered, "Everyone who drinks this water will be thirsty again, ¹⁴ but whoever drinks the water I give them will never thirst. Indeed, the water I give them will become in them a spring of water welling up to eternal life."

¹⁵ The woman said to him, "Sir, give me this water so that I won't get thirsty and have to keep coming here to draw water."

¹⁶ He told her, "Go, call your husband and come back."

¹⁷ "I have no husband," she replied.

Jesus said to her, "You are right when you say you have no husband. [18] The fact is, you have had five husbands, and the man you now have is not your husband. What you have just said is quite true."
[19] "Sir," the woman said, "I can see that you are a prophet.

This is a beautiful story showing how God's love can change a life. The Apostle John tells us that Jesus is traveling from Judea to Galilee and had to go through Samaria. If we look at a map of Israel, we see that Judea is in the south, Galilee is in the north, and Samaria is in between. We would assume that John is simply stating the obvious, but that assumption would be very wrong. Samaria was enemy territory. A good Jew would not travel through Samaria to get to Galilee. Instead, he would head east and follow the Jordan River north. It was a longer route, but that way he would avoid Samaria. Jesus informed his disciples that they **had** to travel through Samaria.

John also tells us that they arrived at Jacob's well at noon. In the Middle East, people do not travel in the afternoon as it is simply too hot. The disciples head into town to get some lunch while Jesus, for some reason, stays at the well. A divine appointment is about to happen, and we discover why Jesus *had* to go through Samaria.

As Jesus is resting by the well, a woman comes to draw water. Once again, in our culture, we would read this as John simply stating facts, but anyone reading this in the first century would be getting a totally different picture. It is very unusual for a woman to be coming to draw water in the afternoon. Women would normally venture out early in the morning, in the cool of the day, to draw water for their families. But this woman, for some reason, arrives at the hottest part of the day. The astute mind of the first century would recognize immediately that this woman is being shunned by her community. She was not to mingle with the respectable women. Later in the story, we discover why she was rejected.

Jesus asks her for a drink. We might see this as quite a simple request. He is thirsty and would like a drink. She has a pitcher and could meet that need. But in asking this of her, he is breaking a number of taboos in that culture. First of all, men did not speak to women. Secondly, a Jew would not talk with a Samaritan (the enemy). Finally, a good Jew would never ask to drink from a Samaritan's pitcher; that would make him unclean according to all the rabbinical teachings of the time. This woman is shocked by the question and answers in such a way to point out all the taboos he is breaking, just in case he is a little ignorant of the culture. *"You are a Jew and I am a Samaritan woman. How can you ask me for a drink?"*

Jesus ignores her question and makes a statement of his own. *"If you knew the gift of God and who it is that asks you for a drink, you would have asked him and he would have given you living water."* The term *living water* is a slight play on words as it also means running water or a fresh stream.

At this point, the woman becomes a little sarcastic. Let me paraphrase her answer. "Where is this fresh stream? Are you wiser than our father Jacob? If there was a fresh stream around, he would not have had to dig this deep well, and we would not have to go through the backbreaking job of hauling the water all the way up from the bottom."

Jesus ignores her comments and goes on to say, *"Everyone who drinks this water will be thirsty again, but whoever drinks the water I give them will never thirst. Indeed, the water I give them will become in them a spring of water welling up to eternal life."* She still has no clue what he is talking about and basically says, "Okay, Mr. Know-it-all. Show me where this stream is so I don't have to keep coming here in the middle of the afternoon to draw water."

Jesus ignores her again and says, *"Go, call your husband and come back."* She truthfully says she has no husband. Then

Jesus firmly but gently replies, *"You are right when you say you have no husband. The fact is, you have had five husbands, and the man you now have is not your husband. What you have just said is quite true."* Now we know why the woman is rejected by her community. She has a very bad reputation.

Sexual sin was a big taboo in that culture. He has just confronted her sin, and yet, she does not feel rejected by this man. How do I know that? Later in the story, we read in verses 28-30, *"Then, leaving her water jar, the woman went back to the town and said to the people, 'Come, see a man who told me everything I ever did. Could this be the Messiah?' They came out of the town and made their way toward him."* She is excited to introduce her community to Jesus. When they knew about her sin, they rejected her. In reading between the lines, I hear her saying something loud and clear, "Come out and meet this man who knows all about me **and still accepts me**. Could this be the Messiah?" Does she sound like she felt rejected by Jesus?

But now, we need to dig deeper to figure out what Jesus was talking about when he spoke of *living water*. He was not talking literally, so what was the analogy he was drawing? As human beings, we tend to see people outwardly. We see their behavior and make judgments. She was living an immoral life, so her community judged and condemned her. Jesus had the amazing ability to see past the outward sin and look inside, seeing the need and the pain. He realized that this woman wanted to be loved. Unfortunately, she started using her body to find love. That is common in our culture as well. Jesus looked inside and saw a well that was very dry. She was *thirsting* for love. Wow, that describes our need perfectly. We all deeply desire to be loved, and many are familiar with that *thirst*.

With that new understanding, let me paraphrase Jesus' comments: "I want you to understand something that is very important. I can quench that thirst with my unconditional love.

69

My love is so great, it will not only fill your life but will overflow like an artesian well. My love is pure love (*agape*), not sexual love (*eros*). Sexual love is conditional; it will not meet your deepest need. My love is the *living water* that you need, and with it, you will never thirst for love again."

How amazing is that! Jesus is saying to us, "If you only knew…" We need to come to know, deep in our inner being, the love of Christ which surpasses all knowledge. If we can grasp this truth, it could change our lives. I believe this woman's life was changed after her encounter with Christ. I see her breaking up with that man who was simply using her for sex and becoming a well-respected member of her community. They also appreciated the fact that she had introduced them to the Messiah, and I have a feeling He changed many lives on that brief stay in Sychar, the place He *had* to go on his journey to Galilee.

ZACCHAEUS THE TAX COLLECTOR
(LUKE 19:1-10)

¹ Jesus entered Jericho and was passing through. ² A man was there by the name of Zacchaeus; he was a chief tax collector and was wealthy. ³ He wanted to see who Jesus was, but because he was short he could not see over the crowd. ⁴ So he ran ahead and climbed a sycamore-fig tree to see him, since Jesus was coming that way.

⁵ When Jesus reached the spot, he looked up and said to him, "Zacchaeus, come down immediately. I must stay at your house today." ⁶ So he came down at once and welcomed him gladly.

⁷ All the people saw this and began to mutter, "He has gone to be the guest of a sinner."

⁸ But Zacchaeus stood up and said to the Lord, "Look, Lord! Here and now I give half of my possessions to the poor, and if I have cheated anybody out of anything, I will pay back four times the amount."

⁹ Jesus said to him, "Today salvation has come to this house, because this man, too, is a son of Abraham. ¹⁰ For the Son of Man came to seek and to save the lost."

I enjoy doing character studies and trying to figure out why people behave as they do. Often, we have a hard time understanding why a person is behaving in a certain way as it does not make sense to us. But, as we recall the subconscious model, we realize that an unhealthy belief, stemming from negative experiences, is driving that behavior. I believe that was true for Zacchaeus. In fact, I have developed a biography about his life and have a feeling I am probably pretty close to the truth. Perhaps I will ask him one day when I reach my heavenly home.

My biography is based on the fact that we are told he was short. I have made the assumption that if he was a small man, he was also a small child. From your experience, how are small children often treated? They are bullied, teased, ridiculed, given hurtful nicknames, etc. I do not think children back in those days were any different from children today. What he was experiencing was hurtful, and all he desired was for others to befriend him. As a teen, he is the 98-pound weakling. Boys continue to bully, and girls make fun of his short stature. The hurt is starting to turn to anger. He becomes a young adult, and that anger is turning to the desire for revenge.

He finds the perfect solution! He becomes a Roman tax collector. Most people stayed away from that occupation as tax collectors were despised, but Zacchaeus felt no one ever loved him anyway. Now, the 98-pound weakling has power! The power of the Roman government on his shoulders.

In our country, we are not that happy to have the Internal Revenue Service do an audit, but it was much worst in that day as the tax collectors were corrupt. Rome was a large empire, controlling conquered nations all over the Middle East and Europe. Tax collectors were hired in each town throughout the empire to collect the taxes for Rome. But Rome did not send out paychecks to the tax collectors. The tax collectors would collect their fee directly from the taxpayer. Gradually, the tax collectors started collecting higher fees than they were entitled to. The problem was, Rome did nothing about it. It seems all they cared about was getting their money; what the tax collector got was his business. Therefore, they were collecting excessive fees, and no one would stop them. The tax collectors were getting rich, and the taxpayers knew they were being cheated. If the taxpayer refused to pay, the tax collector would simply go to the local Roman guards and say, "This man is refusing to pay his tax," and they would haul him off to prison, no questions asked.

Now you know why tax collectors were so despised. That is power. Zacchaeus is getting his revenge! I can just imagine hearing him say to those who had mistreated him: "I remember you. You were in my second-grade class and bullied me every day. Here is what you owe!"

One day, Jesus comes to his town. Jesus is very popular at this time and large crowds are gathered around him as he walks down the main thoroughfare. Here we are told that Zacchaeus is short and cannot see Jesus over the heads of the crowd. Why would he want to see Jesus? My thought is that he wanted to see what Jesus looked like. He was trying to figure out why Jesus was so popular. What makes him special? Was he like those handsome young men that the girls swooned over? Those same girls that made fun of him! He runs ahead and climbs up a tree, so he can see Jesus as he passes by.

Jesus is now approaching the tree and sees Zacchaeus. He knows Zacchaeus in the same way he knew the woman at the well because He is the Messiah. He has divine insight and awareness. But I can imagine him turning to someone beside him and asking, "Who is that man in the tree?" We all know what the answer would be. "That scum of a man is Zacchaeus the tax collector, one of the worst if you know what I mean. Stay far away from him or he'll steal the shirt right off your back!" But what does Jesus do? He walks straight to the tree, looks up and says, *"Zacchaeus, come down immediately. I must stay at your house today."*

Zacchaeus leads Jesus to his home, they walk in together, and Jesus shuts the door behind him, leaving the crowd outside to grumble. I have a feeling that this was the first time anyone had ever set foot in his house. They spend the rest of the day together, talking, eating, and enjoying each other's company. I doubt that Jesus said one thing about Zacchaeus being a tax collector; He simply loved him with God's *agape* love. That love struck a nerve deep inside Zacchaeus. This is what he had always wanted from the time he was a small child. A deep need was being met. The hurt was being healed. At the end of the day, Zacchaeus confesses to Jesus, *"Look, Lord! Here and now I give half of my possessions to the poor, and if I have cheated anybody out of anything, I will pay back four times the amount."* Jesus said to him, *"Today salvation has come to this house, because this man, too, is a son of Abraham. For the Son of Man came to seek and to save the lost."*

That is where the story ends, but that is not the end of my biography. I see him working diligently over the next several days, going over his accounts and making note of everyone he has cheated. Then he starts out and knocks at the door of *Thomas Tax Payer*.

Thomas opens the door, "Oh no. Not you again. Weren't you here last month? How much do you want now?"

Zacchaeus simply says, "Thomas, I have been cheating you, taking more for my fee than I should have. Here, I am returning the money that I wrongly took. I am so sorry, and just to let you know that it will never happen again, here is four times as much. Have a wonderful vacation with your lovely wife." With that said, Zacchaeus walks away.

Thomas shuts the door and shakes his head, *"Did that just happen? I can't believe it. Maybe Zacchaeus is not as bad as I thought."* The next day he sees Zacchaeus walking along the road. He walks up, shakes his hand and says, "Hey Zacchaeus, how are you doing today? My wife is cooking a nice lamb stew, would you like to come over for dinner?" (*philia* is now at work). I can see his whole life turning around after that brief encounter with Jesus.

Yes, much of our sin grows out of our hurt and unmet needs, but the unconditional love of God can turn our lives around and help us become more like Jesus.

CHAPTER 6

EXPERIENCING GOD'S UNCONDITIONAL LOVE

L et us now take what we learned earlier about the subconscious mind and apply it to building the healthy subconscious belief: I am loved unconditionally by God. We have been looking at some scriptures in order to better understand what the Bible teaches about God's love. This is important for empowering the conscious mind and giving it a solid, rational framework before we can enable that truth to begin penetrating the subconscious. We learned earlier that subconscious beliefs change the best through repetition. I must behave in certain ways or think certain thoughts consistently based on rational goals. My goal is to help the subconscious experience God's love.

The question that we have to answer is, "How do I experience God's love?" When Jesus was living on earth, the disciples and those around him were able to experience his love and compassion in the flesh. We saw wonderful examples of how his love transformed two lives in particular, but we know he transformed many other lives as well. Now he resides in heaven. How can we experience his love now?

Twenty years before I learned this subconscious model, something happened that transformed my understanding of God's love. It was during the second semester of my freshman year at college where I was majoring in Christian Education. For one of my classes, I had to purchase a book entitled *Let God Love You*. The book was simply a devotional on the book of Philippians, but I could not get the title out of my head. Every time I saw that title, I felt God saying, "You've never let me love you the way I want to love you." To be honest, it did not make much sense. I grew up in a church that taught God's love. If anyone had asked during my teen years, "Do you know that God loves you?" I would have immediately said, "Yes."

My heart was very open to God at this stage of my life, so even though I was confused, I desired to obey God. I remember thinking, *"How do I let God love me?"* I could only think of two ways, and both involved my morning devotional time. I was in the habit of spending time each morning reading the Bible and praying.

First, I started searching for God's love. I used a concordance to find passages that contained the word love, especially using the Greek word a*gape* (the New Testament was originally written in Greek). I would go to each scripture passage and try to understand what it was saying about God's love.

Next, I began to listen for God's voice during my prayer time. This was new to me. Normally, I just prayed to God and never thought about trying to listen. But now, every time I listened, the first thing I heard was, "Dave, I love you." I would hear other encouraging or affirming words, but those four words always came first. That was happening every time I prayed, no matter if I was in a good or bad mood. After about four months of this, I began to feel God's love in a way I had never felt it before. It was wonderful, and I was experiencing a deeper joy than ever before. Something was happening deep inside.

I remember thinking, *"What did I feel before?"* I thought I knew God's love, but it was nothing like this. As I examined my previous feelings, the words that came to mind were that I felt *God put up with me.* That made sense. When I invited Christ into my life as an eight-year-old child, I believed that I was saved and going to heaven. I never doubted my salvation, and I accepted that as His love. But I still did not like myself, so I saw God as being willing to *put up with me* with all my imperfection and sin. The negative belief that I was unlovable still affected my feelings and made it difficult to feel loved. But of course, God *putting up with me* did not feel like God loving me unconditionally. The subconscious belief had not yet been changed. After four months of daily hearing, "Dave, I love you," something had changed inside, and I was finally able to feel loved.

Twenty years later, the model for the mind helped me understand what had happened. Through the daily repetition, the belief slowly changed from "I am unlovable" to "I am loved by God." The changed subconscious belief affected my deepest feelings, but it had also affected me in another way. As I deeply believed that God loved me, I started liking myself better and believing that others might like me.

Unfortunately, before coming across that model, I gave some poor advice to some of my clients who also found it hard to feel that God loved them.

During my six years in England and the first couple years counseling professionally with Hope Alive Counseling Services, I talked with a number of people who found it difficult to feel God's love. Some would say, "I know God loves me up here (pointing to their head), but I can't feel it down here (pointing to their heart)." At this stage of my life, I still did not fully understand what had happened to me during that first year of college. Here is what I thought happened: *I had let God love me, and by doing so, I had come to deeply feel His love.* My advice to those who struggled to feel God's love was simple. "You need to listen for God's voice and let Him tell you He loves you." Armed with these instructions, my clients would come back with three different answers. A few would say, "I heard God tell me He loves me." I was quick to respond, "Wonderful! Now you need to hear that every day, and eventually, you will begin to feel God's love more fully."

The second answer was more common, "I listened, but I didn't hear anything." How do I respond to that? Were they not listening hard enough?

If that was not bad enough, a third group came back saying, "I listened, but I heard God telling me how bad I am (or other negative messages)." Wow, that backfired! How was I to respond? I led them to think that if they listened, God would speak to them, but they were not hearing God communicating His love.

I soon realized that I was giving advice out of my own spiritual experience, without understanding the dynamics of what had happened to me psychologically. Fortunately, it was during this time that I discovered the model for the mind. Combining this new understanding of the subconscious along with other psychological studies, the pieces began to fit together. I realized that I had consciously chosen to hear God say, "Dave, I love you." Seeing that book title and sensing that God wanted to love me opened me up to hear those words. Hearing those words daily allowed my subconscious to experience it, and repetition enabled the belief to slowly change.

The model helped me understand why my feelings had changed. I then had to admit the reason a few of my clients heard God say, "I love you," was because I had told them God wanted to communicate His love to them. They were prepared to hear those words. Therefore, they also consciously chose to hear God communicate His love.

Now, I understood why many clients listened and heard nothing. It is not a matter of simply opening my mind to hear

God's voice. Yes, He can speak to us in that way, but for most that is a foreign concept.

Those who had a strong belief that they were unlovable were good candidates to hear negative messages. It was not God who was speaking; it was the negative subconscious belief speaking loudly in the silence (just like my second date when my subconscious was loudly telling me, *"She hates my guts and never wants to see me again!"*).

Armed with this new understanding of the psychological dynamics of how to change subconscious beliefs, I wisely adjusted how I guided clients in helping them *hear and experience* God's love. The secret is enabling the Bible, God's Spirit, and the conscious mind to work together to heal the damaged subconscious belief.

We start with the Bible. Many believe, as I do, that the Bible is God's Word. Hebrews 3:1-2 says, *"In the past God spoke to our ancestors through the prophets at many times and in various ways, but in these last days he has spoken to us by his Son."* Another good verse is II Timothy 3:16, *"All Scripture is God-breathed and is useful for teaching, rebuking, correcting and training in righteousness."* Jesus is often referred to as *the living word*. He spoke God's word in the flesh. Now that He is residing in heaven, we are left with *the written word*.

There are many wonderful verses which communicate God's love for mankind. Unfortunately, my conscious mind can believe those truths long before they can penetrate the subconscious. Also, many verses are not personal enough for the subconscious.

Let me illustrate with a wonderful Bible verse,

> *For God so loved the world that he gave his one and only Son, that whoever believes in him shall not perish but have eternal life* (John 3:16).

To the damaged subconscious, the reaction to this verse is, "God loves the world, what does that mean to me?" It is too general for the subconscious. I spoke earlier of a woman who believed God loved everyone else in the world but could not believe God loved her. As I was thinking about this one day after having worked with the subconscious model for a few years, the psychological dynamic of her statement suddenly hit me in the face. She had been a Christian for over 20 years and had heard John 3:16 many times over. Her subconscious firmly believed that *God loved the **world***. The subconscious, which thinks very literally, could accept that God loved the world (a general statement). But when it came to herself specifically, the stubborn "I am unlovable" belief would not let go. The subconscious has to personally experience the truth that *God loves me*!

Therefore, I began instructing my clients to take verses that communicate God's love, study them, and personalize them in a way that enables God to speak those words into their hearts. Let us take John 3:16. My conscious mind can think rationally and abstractly. I can see that God deeply loves the world, and understand that means every human being *including myself*. Now I can rephrase the verse like this, "Dave, I love you so much that I sent my only Son to sacrifice His life for you on the cross, so that you can put your faith in Him and become a part of My family and live with Me forever." Now, try it using your name. How does that feel? These words contain the truth being communicated in John 3:16, but now I have something personal to memorize and hear. I can now choose to hear God's voice and be confident that it is God's word. I can let the Holy Spirit speak those words into my heart (by consciously thinking the words), and the *written word* once again becomes the *living word*. My subconscious can experience God's wonderful love over and over until it firmly believes that I am loved unconditionally by God. Feel free to discover other verses that you can personalize to convey God's wonderful love for you.

By the way, after four months of hearing God say, "Dave, I love you," it had become a habit. Therefore, it continues to be a special part of my devotional time over forty years later, and I never get tired of hearing those words!

FINAL THOUGHTS ABOUT GOD'S LOVE

I realize that some reading this book may not be very familiar with the Bible. Perhaps you have not even gone to church, and some of what I am saying does not make sense. You may be asking, "What do you mean when you speak of Christ sacrificing himself on the cross, or praying a prayer of salvation, or having a personal relationship with God?"

I would like to share with you what the Bible calls "the Gospel", which, translated into English, simply means "Good News!" The Old Testament contained the stories of God dealing with His people the Israelites. All through the Old Testament, there were prophecies of a coming Messiah who would reign as the King of the World. Isaiah 9:6 beautifully portrays this:

> *For to us a child is born, to us a son is given, and*
> *the government will be on his shoulders. And he will*
> *be called Wonderful Counselor, Mighty God,*
> *Everlasting Father, Prince of Peace.*

Jesus Christ is that Messiah. The New Testament is all about him. He is described as God incarnate, or God in the flesh. God somehow planted an embryo in a young virgin named Mary, who was engaged to Joseph. Jesus was born as the unique God/man of history who had no sin in his life. The name "Jesus" means *God saves*. He represented God perfectly to mankind while he lived on earth, but ultimately his mission was to give His life as a sacrifice for our sin on the cross. The Bible teaches that on the cross, Jesus took our sin upon Himself and paid the penalty for that sin. He offers His righteousness to us in return so that we can receive salvation as a gift of His love and grace. But you might be wondering, *"How do we receive this salvation?"*

Here are a few verses, all referring to Jesus, to help answer this important question (we have already looked at the first one):

> *For God so loved the world that he gave his one and only Son, that whoever believes in him shall not perish but have eternal life* (John 3:16).

> *For I am not ashamed of the gospel, because it is the power of God that brings salvation to everyone who believes: first to the Jew, then to the Gentile* (Romans 1:16).

> *Salvation is found in no one else, for there is no other name under heaven given to mankind by which we must be saved* (Acts 4:12).

> *If we confess our sins, he is faithful and just and will forgive us our sins and purify us from all unrighteousness* (I John 1:8).

> *If you declare with your mouth, "Jesus is Lord," and believe in your heart that God raised him from the dead, you will be saved. For it is with your heart that you believe and are justified, and it is with your mouth that you profess your faith and are saved* (Romans 10:9-10).

For it is by grace you have been saved, through faith—and this is not from yourselves, it is the gift of God—not by works, so that no one can boast (Ephesians 2:8-9).

Therefore, there is now no condemnation for those who are in Christ Jesus, because through Christ Jesus the law of the Spirit who gives life has set you free from the law of sin and death (Romans 8:1-2).

These verses explain that we must believe (a conscious process) that Jesus Christ died on the cross for our sin. We can then confess our sin to God (which is declaring that we are genuinely sorry for those sins and asking God to forgive us) and receive His gift of salvation by inviting him into our lives as Lord and Savior, thereby committing our lives to him. We then become a part of God's family, and all our sin is forgiven.

I like to compare it to marriage. Marriage also is an act of commitment. We commit our life to another person and become a family. Likewise, the Bible says we are Christ's bride. Revelation 19:7 says, *"Let us rejoice and be glad and give him glory! For the wedding of the Lamb (Jesus) has come, and his bride has made herself ready."* On the cross, Jesus paid the penalty for our sin and invited us to become his bride. We must say "yes" to this invitation, at which point we become his bride, and He covers us with His robe of righteousness. Our sins are forgiven, and we become part of God's family forever. God is our Father, and He adopts us as His beloved children. If that is not good news, I do not know what is!

Our "yes" can come in different ways, but the most common is simply a prayer of commitment, similar to what I prayed at the altar of our church that Sunday morning as an eight-year-old child. Here is a sample prayer you could pray:

"Father, I thank you for sending Jesus Christ into this world to give His life as a sacrifice for my sin. I am truly sorry for my sin and bad deeds, and I desire to change and live for you. I receive You into my life as Lord and Savior. Today I make this commitment: to live in a close relationship with You and to allow You to transform my life from the inside out through Your wonderful love and grace. Amen."

If you say this to God, and mean it from the depths of your heart, you are now a part of God's wonderful family. You can spend the rest of your life in an intimate relationship with God and continue to get to know Him better each day as you read the Bible and pray. He may need to work on your self-image as He did mine. Believe me, you will like the changes He makes.

CHAPTER 7

NEED NUMBER TWO
THE NEED TO BE VALUED

THE UNHEALTHY BELIEF:
I AM WORTHLESS

SYMPTOMS OF THE BELIEF

- Feeling useless or lacking purpose
- Feeling stupid or lazy
- Thinking, *"I am not very talented, smart, or creative. What good am I?"*
- Lying to enhance self-importance
- Thinking, *"If I weren't around, what difference would it make"*
- Apologizing constantly
- Avoiding new tasks or challenges
- Fearing failure
- Feeling inferior to others
- Not taking risks to see my potential
- Behaving self-destructively

The belief that I am worthless or useless is actually quite common. Many of us have experienced being put down or belittled as children. Family members or other adults may have made fun of your lack of coordination or skills even though you were not old enough to have developed good coordination or skills. You may have been called stupid, lazy, or good for nothing. Such words cut deep into the heart of a child and are believed. This belief can create a fear of failure, which keeps us from launching out and discovering our full potential. Each time we make a mistake, we prove to ourselves that we are unable to succeed. We envy people who are talented, athletic, mechanically gifted, successful, famous, etc. They are the people who have value, not me. Remember, the negative belief can be mild, moderate, or strong. The stronger the belief, the greater the symptoms.

One of the problems is that people value us conditionally. We are valued because of our capabilities, talents, attractiveness, success, etc. Unfortunately, we tend to devalue ourselves because we can always find others who appear better than us in some way.

We all have a deep need to feel that our life has value or purpose. When we struggle to feel valuable, there is a degree of emptiness or lack of fulfillment in our lives. I was aware of these symptoms in my life as a teenager, especially as it related to God. I felt useless as a Christian. That is why I felt such joy when I was singing in that youth choir. I was doing something useful, even if it was simply sharing Christ's love within a thirty-member choir. But once again, the deeper esteem need is to be valued simply because I am.

THE HEALTHY BELIEF:
I AM VALUED UNCONDITIONALLY BY GOD

It is quite common to believe God values us conditionally as well. We develop beliefs about God long before we get to know the Bible. Why should God be any different from people? We might think, *"God greatly valued a godly man like the late Rev. Billy Graham. I could never measure up to that. God probably doesn't even notice me."* What if I said that you are as valuable to God as Billy Graham? Would you believe me? Well, that is the truth. God is very different than people. Once again, we need the Bible to help us understand who God is and how He sees us. The best place to start is the beginning.

CREATION (GENESIS 1)

[1] In the beginning God created the heavens and the earth. [2] Now the earth was formless and empty, darkness was over the surface of the deep, and the Spirit of God was hovering over the waters.

*[3] And God said, "Let there be light," and there was light. [4] God saw that **the light was good**, and he separated the light from the darkness. [5] God called the light "day," and the darkness he called "night." And there was evening, and there was morning—the first day.*

[6] And God said, "Let there be a vault between the waters to separate water from water." [7] So God made the vault and separated the water under the vault from the water above it. And it was so. [8] God called the vault "sky." And there was evening, and there was morning—the second day.

[9] And God said, "Let the water under the sky be gathered to one place, and let dry ground appear."

*And it was so. [10] God called the dry ground "land," and the gathered waters he called "seas." And God saw that **it was good**.*

*[11] Then God said, "Let the land produce vegetation: seed-bearing plants and trees on the land that bear fruit with seed in it, according to their various kinds." And it was so. [12] The land produced vegetation: plants bearing seed according to their kinds and trees bearing fruit with seed in it according to their kinds. And God saw that **it was good**. [13] And there was evening, and there was morning—the third day.*

*[14] And God said, "Let there be lights in the vault of the sky to separate the day from the night, and let them serve as signs to mark sacred times, and days and years, [15] and let them be lights in the vault of the sky to give light on the earth." And it was so. [16] God made two great lights—the greater light to govern the day and the lesser light to govern the night. He also made the stars. [17] God set them in the vault of the sky to give light on the earth, [18] to govern the day and the night, and to separate light from darkness. And God saw that **it was good**. [19] And there was evening, and there was morning—the fourth day.*

*[20] And God said, "Let the water teem with living creatures, and let birds fly above the earth across the vault of the sky." [21] So God created the great creatures of the sea and every living thing with which the water teems and that moves about in it, according to their kinds, and every winged bird according to its kind. And God saw that **it was good**. [22] God blessed them and said, "Be fruitful and increase in number and fill the water in the seas, and let the birds increase on the earth." [23] And there was evening, and there was morning—the fifth day.*

*²⁴ And God said, "Let the land produce living creatures according to their kinds: the livestock, the creatures that move along the ground, and the wild animals, each according to its kind." And it was so. ²⁵ God made the wild animals according to their kinds, the livestock according to their kinds, and all the creatures that move along the ground according to their kinds. And God saw that **it was good.***

²⁶ Then God said, "Let us make mankind in our image, in our likeness, so that they may rule over the fish in the sea and the birds in the sky, over the livestock and all the wild animals, and over all the creatures that move along the ground."

²⁷ So God created mankind in his own image, in the image of God he created them; male and female he created them.

²⁸ God blessed them and said to them, "Be fruitful and increase in number; fill the earth and subdue it. Rule over the fish in the sea and the birds in the sky and over every living creature that moves on the ground."

²⁹ Then God said, "I give you every seed-bearing plant on the face of the whole earth and every tree that has fruit with seed in it. They will be yours for food. ³⁰ And to all the beasts of the earth and all the birds in the sky and all the creatures that move along the ground—everything that has the breath of life in it—I give every green plant for food." And it was so.

*³¹ God saw all that he had made, and **it was very good.** And there was evening, and there was morning—the sixth day.*
(Genesis 1:1-31 – emphasis mine)

The creation story at the beginning of the Bible is beautifully written. God is the all-powerful great creator. Each day God created something new. At the end of each day, He viewed His creation and said, *"It is good."* Everything that God creates is good. But notice that on the sixth day, after God created man, He says something slightly different, *"It is very good."* Man was the greatest of God's creation because man was created in God's image.

Genesis 2:7 adds another aspect of the creation of man which reveals how we were created in God's image, *"The LORD God formed a man from the dust of the ground and breathed into his nostrils the breath of life, and the man became a living being."*

The word for breath in Hebrew (the original language of the Old Testament) is *Ruach.* This Hebrew word can also be translated as wind or spirit. When God created man, he was flesh and blood, like any animal. Then *God breathed into man.* This could also be translated as *God placed His Spirit inside man.* We are not just flesh, we are also spiritual beings. That is how we are created in *the image of God.* The spirit of man is everlasting, and it is through the spirit that we can commune and have a relationship with God. He loves all of His creation but desires a relationship with man. We are especially valuable to God. Jesus communicates this same truth in two key verses in the New Testament.

> *True worshipers will worship the Father in the Spirit and in truth, for they are the kind of worshipers the Father seeks. God is spirit, and his worshipers must worship in the Spirit and in truth* (John 4:23-24).

> *Look at the birds of the air; they do not sow or reap or store away in barns, and yet your heavenly Father feeds them. Are you not much more valuable than they?* (Matthew 6:26).

We are able to worship God because we are spiritual beings. God loves and values the animals because he created them, but He is *our* heavenly Father. We are not just more valuable than the animals, we are *much* more valuable. God is our Father, a perfect Father who treasures us and values us because we are His children.

THE BEGINNING OF EVIL

You might be asking at this point, "If everything God creates is good, how did evil come into the world? The Bible also speaks of the devil and demons. Did God create them?" This is important because it is also associated with another question I have had many clients ask, "If God really loves and values me, why did He allow bad things to happen to me?" And believe me, I have had clients who have had some very bad things happen. It is not easy to answer these questions, but I believe a healthy understanding of the Bible can at least let us know that God does love and value us, even though there is evil in the world.

I can best answer these questions by helping us understand a very important theological principle, *free will*. God's love requires that spiritual beings be free to choose – free to love and obey God or free to reject and disobey God. Free will includes all spiritual beings, human and angelic.

There are two Old Testament passages which help answer the question, "Why is there a devil who is also called Satan?" We will begin with Ezekiel 28:11-19:

> [11] *The word of the LORD came to me:* [12] *"Son of man, take up a lament concerning the king of Tyre and say to him: 'This is what the Sovereign LORD says:*
> *"'You were the seal of perfection,*
> *full of wisdom and perfect in beauty.*
> [13] *You were in Eden,*

the garden of God;
every precious stone adorned you:
    carnelian, chrysolite and emerald,
    topaz, onyx and jasper,
    lapis lazuli, turquoise and beryl.
Your settings and mountings were made of gold;
    on the day you were created they were prepared.
14 You were anointed as a guardian cherub,
    for so I ordained you.
You were on the holy mount of God;
    you walked among the fiery stones.
15 You were blameless in your ways
    from the day you were created
    till wickedness was found in you.
16 Through your widespread trade
    you were filled with violence,
    and you sinned.
So I drove you in disgrace from the mount of God,
    and I expelled you, guardian cherub,
    from among the fiery stones.
17 Your heart became proud
    on account of your beauty,
and you corrupted your wisdom
    because of your splendor.
So I threw you to the earth;
    I made a spectacle of you before kings.
18 By your many sins and dishonest trade
    you have desecrated your sanctuaries.
So I made a fire come out from you,
    and it consumed you,
and I reduced you to ashes on the ground
    in the sight of all who were watching.
19 All the nations who knew you
    are appalled at you;

you have come to a horrible end
and will be no more.

This is a lament concerning the King of Tyre. The previous lament in Ezekiel 28:1-10 was also concerning the King of Tyre. There we read in verse 2 that the King of Tyre became proud and said, *"I am a god."* Many scholars believe that in this second lament, Ezekiel is switching to another spiritual being who became proud. An angelic being who also wanted to be a god and was thrown out of heaven. The passage says that he was *in Eden*. Genesis tells of the devil tempting Eve in the Garden of Eden. (We will look at that story later.) The angel described here was *perfect, full of wisdom and beauty*. Most likely, the greatest and most powerful of all the angels God created. It says he *was blameless until wickedness entered* his life. He became proud *because of his beauty and splendor*.
Next, we look at Isaiah 14:12-17:

[12]How you have fallen from heaven,
morning star, son of the dawn!
You have been cast down to the earth,
you who once laid low the nations!
[13] You said in your heart,
"I will ascend to the heavens;
I will raise my throne
above the stars of God;
I will sit enthroned on the mount of assembly,
on the utmost heights of Mount Zaphon.
[14] I will ascend above the tops of the clouds;
I will make myself like the Most High."
[15] But you are brought down to the realm of the dead,
to the depths of the pit.
[16] Those who see you stare at you,
they ponder your fate:
"Is this the man who shook the earth

> *and made kingdoms tremble,*
> *¹⁷ the man who made the world a wilderness,*
> *who overthrew its cities*
> *and would not let his captives go home?*

Here we see the name of this powerful angel that fell from heaven: *Morning Star,* which is the English translation of the Hebrew name *Lucifer.* This passage is often called "the five I wills of Lucifer." Lucifer, a beautiful angel, the greatest and most powerful of all the angels, became proud and said, *I will become like the Most High.* He actually believed that he could conquer God and was able to gather a large host of angels to lead a rebellion against God. But he was no match for God and was thrown out of heaven. The Bible says that hell was created for the devil and his followers (Matthew 25:41). We see that God did not create the devil or demons. They came about because of free will. They <u>chose</u> to rebel.

This also answers the question, "Why is there evil in the world?" Here we go back to the beginning and look at the story of the fall of man in Genesis 3.

> *¹ Now the serpent was more crafty than any of the wild animals the LORD God had made. He said to the woman, "Did God really say, 'You must not eat from any tree in the garden'?"*
> *² The woman said to the serpent, "We may eat fruit from the trees in the garden, ³ but God did say, 'You must not eat fruit from the tree that is in the middle of the garden, and you must not touch it, or you will die.'"*
> *⁴ "You will not certainly die," the serpent said to the woman. ⁵ "For God knows that when you eat from it your eyes will be opened, and you will be like God, knowing good and evil."*

6 When the woman saw that the fruit of the tree was good for food and pleasing to the eye, and also desirable for gaining wisdom, she took some and ate it. She also gave some to her husband, who was with her, and he ate it. 7 Then the eyes of both of them were opened, and they realized they were naked; so they sewed fig leaves together and made coverings for themselves.

8 Then the man and his wife heard the sound of the LORD God as he was walking in the garden in the cool of the day, and they hid from the LORD God among the trees of the garden. 9 But the LORD God called to the man, "Where are you?"

10 He answered, "I heard you in the garden, and I was afraid because I was naked; so I hid."

11 And he said, "Who told you that you were naked? Have you eaten from the tree that I commanded you not to eat from?"

12 The man said, "The woman you put here with me—she gave me some fruit from the tree, and I ate it."

13 Then the LORD God said to the woman, "What is this you have done?"

The woman said, "The serpent deceived me, and I ate."

14 So the LORD God said to the serpent, "Because you have done this,

"Cursed are you above all livestock and all wild animals!
You will crawl on your belly and you will eat dust all the days of your life.
15 And I will put enmity between you and the woman, and between your offspring and hers;

> *he will crush your head,*
> *and you will strike his heel.* "
> [16] *To the woman he said,*
> *"I will make your pains in childbearing very severe;*
> *with painful labor you will give birth to children.*
> *Your desire will be for your husband,*
> *and he will rule over you.* "
> [17] *To Adam he said, "Because you listened to your*
> *wife and ate fruit from the tree about which I*
> *commanded you, 'You must not eat from it,'*
> *"Cursed is the ground because of you;*
> *through painful toil you will eat food from it*
> *all the days of your life.*
> [18] *It will produce thorns and thistles for you,*
> *and you will eat the plants of the field.*
> [19] *By the sweat of your brow*
> *you will eat your food*
> *until you return to the ground,*
> *since from it you were taken;*
> *for dust you are*
> *and to dust you will return* (Genesis 3:1-19).

At the beginning of this chapter, we find Adam and Eve enjoying the beautiful garden God had created for them. Judging by the boundaries listed in Genesis, theologians have estimated the Garden of Eden to be around 1,500 square miles. That is larger than the state of Rhode Island, one huge garden paradise. In the second chapter of Genesis, we learn that Adam had the privilege of naming all the animals (Genesis 2:20). God let Adam and Eve know they could enjoy everything in the garden except the tree in the middle of the garden which He called the tree of *the knowledge of good and evil*. They were told that if they ate of that tree, they would die (Genesis 2:17). With that declaration, free will enters the picture.

Without that choice, there is no free will. How could they choose to disobey if there was nothing to disobey?

When we examine this, God made it very easy to obey. Enjoy everything in 1,500 square miles of paradise and live, or eat from one little tree and die. We have no idea how long they had been living in the garden by the time we get to Genesis 3. It could have been hundreds of years. Death had not yet entered the world, and without death, they could live forever in the paradise God had given them. To be honest, I do not believe that Adam and Eve got anywhere near that tree. They believed God and did not want to die. Why do I think that? Well, let us proceed with the story.

The serpent enters the picture. We know from the context that this was Satan himself, the great deceiver, who had been cast out of heaven and was present on earth. He approaches Eve one day and asks, *"Did God really say, 'You must not eat from any tree in the garden'?"* He knows the answer but he is cleverly manipulating her thinking. Let me paraphrase Eve's answer. "Of course, not! God lets us eat from all these wonderful, delicious trees." Then almost as if in an afterthought she says, "Oh yes, there is one tree, somewhere in the middle of the garden. God said not to eat or even touch that tree or we will die." I know I am taking some liberty with my paraphrase, and it is only my perspective, but please humor me for a moment as I make a point. Notice that she goes beyond what God actually said. He said not to eat of the tree. She added, "…we are not to touch it." They believed God and did not want to get anywhere near that evil tree. They did not want to die.

The trap was set. Satan answers boldly and firmly, *"You will not certainly die, for God knows that when you eat from it your eyes will be opened, and you will be like God, knowing good and evil."* He has just called God a liar and given her a reason for the lie. If Adam and Eve would eat from that tree, instead of dying, they would become as great and powerful as

God. He was implying that God was trying to keep them subservient by not allowing them to eat from that tree. Satan most likely thought that the same thinking which tempted him to rebel would be a temptation to man as well.

The next verse says, *"The woman saw that the fruit of the tree was good for food and pleasing to the eye."* Here is where I get the idea that Adam and Eve had stayed far from that tree. The implication is that this is the first time Eve has ever looked at the tree, and it **looked good**. Not only did it look good, but it could make her as wise and powerful as God.

Now, please give me some more liberty with the text. I do not think she ate of the tree immediately after Satan tempted her. I know human nature and temptation pretty well. I believe, at that moment, a battle began in her mind. "Is God lying to us? No, He has been so good to us! But is he trying to prevent us from becoming wise and powerful? Surely not! But perhaps? No. But..." I can see her battling for months. Finally, the temptation becomes too great. She grabs the fruit and takes a bite. She cringes but does not die. Maybe the serpent was right. She gives the fruit to Adam. He is uncertain but also takes a bite. He does not die either.

But then their eyes are opened and they realize they are naked. Sin and shame had entered the world, and they did die, just not in the way they had anticipated. The spirit, the breath of God inside them, died. They had disobeyed God, and everything changed. Then they slowly began to age because no one would ever want to live forever in a sinful fallen world. Think about it. Would you want to live forever in this world of sin and pain? I doubt it. A lifetime is too much for many who have suffered greatly in this world.

Just as Lucifer was thrown out of heaven, Adam and Eve were thrown out of paradise to work and toil in order to get food and survive to the best of their ability.

Another way to understand the *death* Adam and Eve experienced in the fall is to see it as spiritual death rather than physical death. Spiritual death can be defined as separation from God. When Adam and Eve ate the fruit of the tree of the knowledge of good and evil, they lost their connection with God. That close intimacy they had with God was now broken. If we use the marriage analogy again, it is as if they divorced themselves from God. Now that they chose to sin, they had no way to reconnect with God. They lost their innocence. Sin was the *virus* that would infect the whole world. The Apostle Paul said it very clearly in Romans 3:23, *"for all have sinned and fall short of the glory of God."*

Even worse, with the fall, Satan gained more power on earth. This opened a Pandora's box of evil. The devil is described as the *"ruler of the kingdom of the air, the spirit who is now at work in those who are disobedient"* (Ephesians 2:2).

All the evil in the world did not come from God. Instead, it came from man deciding to be disobedient, and Satan taking advantage of that in order to make our lives miserable and ultimately destroy us. In referring to Satan, John 10:10 tells us, *"the thief comes only to steal and kill and destroy."* All that God creates is good. Man allowed evil to enter the world.

If man had not been very valuable to God, He would have had a pretty easy decision about what to do next. He would have simply thought: *"Man decided he didn't want me. That's fine. I will just leave him to his own fate, head to some other galaxy, prepare another planet suitable for life, and try again."* I would shudder to think what would have happened to man if God had abandoned us. I can guarantee you we would have never made it to the 21st Century!

CHAPTER 8

THE CROSS

Fortunately for us, that is not what happened. We were so valuable to God that from the beginning of time, He had established a Plan B. Man was cast out of the Garden of Eden but was not immediately condemned eternally to hell as Lucifer was. Instead, man was allowed to continue to dwell on earth, but that will not continue forever. The Bible indicates that this world will come to an end one day. But that has not happened yet, and until then we all have a chance to be *reconciled* to God. Lucifer was not given a plan of redemption, only man.

Plan B enables fallen man to once again have a choice, on an individual basis, to reestablish a relationship with God. Jesus Christ and the cross comprise this plan of redemption or reconciliation. I quoted the first part of John 10:10 to show us that the devil wants to destroy us, but let me share the whole verse with you:

> *The thief (Satan) comes only to steal and kill and destroy; I (Jesus) have come that they may have life, and have it to the full.*

Sin produces spiritual death. We are separated from God at birth because of the sin of Adam. But Jesus Christ, who is called the last Adam (I Corinthians 15:49), came to restore spiritual life (life in relationship with God). Notice, Jesus not only restores a relationship with God but desires to give us a full (abundant or whole) life.

One of the reasons I believe the Bible, especially the plan of redemption through the cross of Christ, is simply because I do not think man could have ever imagined it, even in his wildest dreams. It goes against everything that man naturally thinks about God. Let me explain.

I have had a lifetime to talk with people about God. In counseling, I am blessed in being able to go beneath the surface and understand how they think and feel, especially about God. If I could sum it all up, most people, without a knowledge of the New Testament (sometimes, even with a knowledge of the New Testament) tend to describe God and salvation something like this:

> We are all imperfect. We do good and bad things.
> My goal in life is to try to do more good things than bad.
> I believe God is a fair judge, and if I can succeed in
> doing more good than bad, surely He will allow me to
> enter heaven. I sure hope so anyway.

I know this is very simplistic, but even though it may be said in many different ways, it all tends to boil down to an attempt to earn God's favor through our good behavior. Why is that? Because this is the way people relate to us, and the way we relate to others. We all have subconscious beliefs about what it means to be a "good person." Our subconscious judges other people's behavior, and if they pass the good person test, we accept them. If not, we subtly, or sometimes not so subtly, show our disdain. Why should God be any different? We tend to see God according to what we have experienced in this world. Some people work hard to try to be good enough.

Others simply feel that they could never be good enough and do not even try.

Most religions around the world are based on a similar philosophy. Salvation must be earned. Each religion may have different ideas about what must be done to earn God's favor, but once we learn what we are to do, we are to do that to the best of our ability. But sadly, with this philosophy, heaven is never a certainty because we never know if we have been good enough for God to accept us.

Now, let us contrast this to what the New Testament teaches about sin, salvation, and heaven. We will see that it is the opposite of what man naturally thinks.

First of all, in God's eyes, there are no *good people* or *bad people*. There are only *sinful people* or *lost people*. He puts us all in the same boat, and we are lost at sea, never able to find our way to God through our own goodness. The Apostle Paul describes this the best in Romans 3:9-23:

> *⁹We have already made the charge that Jews and Gentiles alike are all under the power of sin. ¹⁰ As it is written:*
> *"There is no one righteous, not even one;*
> *¹¹ there is no one who understands;*
> *there is no one who seeks God.*
> *¹² All have turned away,*
> *they have together become worthless;*
> *there is no one who does good,*
> *not even one."*
> *¹³ "Their throats are open graves;*
> *their tongues practice deceit."*
> *"The poison of vipers is on their lips."*
> *¹⁴ "Their mouths are full of cursing and bitterness."*
> *¹⁵ "Their feet are swift to shed blood;*
> *¹⁶ ruin and misery mark their ways,*

17 and the way of peace they do not know."

18 "There is no fear of God before their eyes."

19 Now we know that whatever the law says, it says to those who are under the law, so that every mouth may be silenced and the whole world held accountable to God. 20 Therefore no one will be declared righteous in God's sight by the works of the law; rather, through the law we become conscious of our sin.

21 But now apart from the law the righteousness of God has been made known, to which the Law and the Prophets testify. 22 This righteousness is given through faith in Jesus Christ to all who believe. There is no difference between Jew and Gentile, 23 for all have sinned and fall short of the glory of God.

Paul makes it very clear, we are all sinners separated from a holy God. That sounds very depressing. What hope does any of us have of going to heaven? This is why the main message of the Gospel is so vitally important. Salvation, according to the New Testament, is not something I can *earn*, it can only be received as a *free gift*! Here are a few verses to help you see this vital truth:

*8 For it is by grace you have been saved, through faith—and this is not from yourselves, it is the **gift** of God— 9 not by works, so that no one can boast* (Ephesians 2:8-9 – emphasis mine).

*14 Nevertheless, death reigned from the time of Adam to the time of Moses, even over those who did not sin by breaking a command, as did Adam, who is a pattern of the one to come. 15 But the **gift** is not like the trespass. For if the many died by the trespass of the one man (Adam), how much more did God's grace and the **gift** that came by the grace of the one man, Jesus*

Christ, overflow to the many! [16] *Nor can the **gift** of God be compared with the result of one man's sin: The judgment followed one sin and brought condemnation, but the **gift** followed many trespasses and brought justification.* [17] *For if, by the trespass of the one man, death reigned through that one man, how much more will those who receive God's abundant provision of grace and of the **gift** of righteousness reign in life through the one man, Jesus Christ!* [18] *Consequently, just as one trespass resulted in condemnation for all people, so also one righteous act resulted in justification and life for all people* (Romans 5:14-18 – emphasis mine).

[21] *But now apart from the law the righteousness of God has been made known, to which the Law and the Prophets testify.* [22] *This righteousness is given through faith in Jesus Christ to all who believe. There is no difference between Jew and Gentile,* [23] *for all have sinned and fall short of the glory of God,* [24] *and all are justified freely by his grace through the redemption that came by Christ Jesus* (Romans 3:21-24).

*For the wages of sin is death, but the **gift** of God is eternal life in Christ Jesus our Lord* (Romans 6:23 – emphasis mine).

Why would God offer heaven to us as a free gift? You are probably thinking, *"Surely there must be some catch. As you know, there is nothing free in this world. It sounds too good to be true."*

You are right, salvation is not free. In fact, it is very costly. *"That's what I figured. There is nothing free. What does God want, my firstborn son?"* But this is where the crazy part of the story comes into play (at least crazy from our perspective).

105

God paid the price for our salvation through Jesus Christ and His death on the cross! It is free to us, but cost God *His* only Son!

Allow me to examine this more closely with you, and then we will look at the Bible to support this wonderful truth. As we have already said, Jesus Christ is the Messiah, the promised Savior predicted in the Old Testament. He came into this world to save the world from sin and death. He ultimately came to offer his life as a sacrifice for our sin. He died on the cross not as a martyr, but as an atoning sacrifice for our sin. This is the amazing message of the Gospel. The Bible communicates that on the cross Jesus took our sin upon himself, paid the penalty for that sin, and offers his righteousness to us as a gift of his love. He gets our sin; we get his righteousness. As a result, God can see us through the righteousness of Christ, and the relationship between God and man can be reestablished.

Now you're thinking, *"Wow, Jesus got the raw end of that deal. Why would he ever do that for us?"* The answer is simple. He loves and values us that much! Here are some scriptures to let you know that I did not make this up. All of the following verses are referring to Jesus.

He is the atoning sacrifice for our sins, and not only for ours but also for the sins of the whole world (I John 2:2).

For Christ also suffered once for sins, the righteous for the unrighteous, to bring you to God. He was put to death in the body but made alive in the Spirit (I Peter 3:18).

⁶Who, being in very nature God,
  did not consider equality with God something to be used to his own advantage;
⁷ rather, he made himself nothing

by taking the very nature of a servant,
being made in human likeness.
⁸ And being found in appearance as a man,
he humbled himself
by becoming obedient to death—
even death on a cross! (Philippians 2:6-8).

But God demonstrates his own love for us in this:
While we were still sinners, Christ died for us
(Romans 5:8).

For this reason he had to be made like them, fully
human in every way, in order that he might become a
merciful and faithful high priest in service to God, and
that he might make atonement for the sins of the
people (Hebrews 2:17).

¹² But when this priest had offered for all time one
sacrifice for sins, he sat down at the right hand of
God, ¹³ and since that time he waits for his enemies to
be made his footstool. ¹⁴ For by one sacrifice he has
made perfect forever those who are being made holy
(Hebrews 10:12-14).

He himself bore our sins in his body on the
cross, so that we might die to sins and live for
righteousness; "by his wounds you have been healed"
(I Peter 2:24).

God made him who had no sin to be sin for us, so
that in him we might become the righteousness of God
(II Corinthians 5:21).

> *This is love: not that we loved God, but that he*
> *loved us and sent his Son as an atoning sacrifice for*
> *our sins* (I John 4:10).

Even though this sounds incredibly amazing, you may, in a small way, be able to understand. Have you ever loved someone so much, perhaps your children or spouse, that you honestly felt that you would be willing to sacrifice your life for them? If you have, then you have a little idea of what Jesus did for us. But you have to multiply your love by infinity to imagine God being willing to give His Son and Jesus being willing to come into this world to sacrifice His life for every person who has ever lived.

Do you now understand why I believe that man would have never come up with this plan of salvation? It had to be God's idea because only His love is great enough to devise such a plan. Also, God was the only one who knew that we could never be good enough to get back to God on our own. The debt of sin had to be paid.

GETTING THIS TRUTH INTO THE SUBCONSCIOUS

Now, we focus again on getting this truth into the subconscious. I can say, "I am valued unconditionally by God," but it is hard to imagine what that feels like. We are usually valued because of something, and many of us feel that we have very little value. We looked at the Bible to see two main truths: God created us, and He gave His life for us through Jesus Christ. You might be saying, "That makes sense, I can logically see that God must value me if He was willing to do that, but I struggle to feel valuable."

Comparisons, analogies, and similes help us understand complex truths. They can also emotionally affect us, and this emotional aspect can help penetrate the subconscious. Jesus often spoke in parables, starting with the phrase, *the Kingdom of God is like...,* in order to help us understand complex spiritual truths.

Therefore, I would like to share several analogies in the hope that you will be able to say, "Yes, I understand, I am valuable to God." You may have to live with the concepts for a while, but allow them to sink deeper and deeper as they come to memory.

THE DEBT HAS BEEN PAID IN FULL

A beautiful analogy comes from the Apostle Paul's letter to the Colossians. Unfortunately, if you do not live in the first century AD, you do not understand the analogy. And if you don't understand the analogy, the emotional impact is lost. It takes some research to fully understand these verses:

> *13 When you were dead in your sins and in the uncircumcision of your flesh, God made you alive with Christ. He forgave us all our sins, 14 having canceled the charge of our legal indebtedness, which stood against us and condemned us; he has taken it away, nailing it to the cross. 15 And having disarmed the powers and authorities, he made a public spectacle of them, triumphing over them by the cross* (Colossians 2:13-15).

What in the world is Paul talking about when he speaks of *the charge of our legal indebtedness*? That phrase in the Greek New Testament is one word, *kerigraphon*. Literally translated it is *"handwriting"* (*keri* means hand, and *graphon* means writing). In fact, that is how it is translated in the King James Version. You may be wondering, *"Why is it translated so differently in the New International Version?"* The New International Version took advantage of the historical context of this word to give us a conceptual translation. In other words, this translation is trying to help us understand what the word meant to a first-century reader.

Anyone reading this verse in the first century would immediately get the analogy. The debtor's prison was well known and quite common in Paul's day. Anyone who owed a debt they could not pay would be placed in the debtor's prison if the lender made that demand. The lender most likely believed that he would never be repaid and wanted the debtor punished.

The debtor could not make any money in prison to pay the debt, so if the debt was substantial, he would most likely spend the rest of his life in prison, separated from society. On the door of the prison was nailed a handwritten list of all the debts owed, so anyone passing by would know why he was imprisoned. Everyone knew what that list of debts was called. You probably have already guessed the answer. It was called the *kerigraphon*. Now, these verses start to make a little more sense. Paul was using the analogy of the debtor's prison.

Paul is comparing our sin to debt. Sin separates us from God, and we have no way of paying the debt, which means we are forever separated from God, just like that debtor is forever separated from society. In fact, there was only one way a debtor could get out of prison. Someone else would have to pay the debt in full. If that happened, they would take the *kerigraphon* (certificate of debt) down from the prison door and write across it in bold lettering, *tetelestai,* which meant, "Paid in full." They would then open the prison door, hand the *kerigraphon* to the prisoner, and he was free to leave. If anyone would question why he was free, he would simply pull out the *kerigraphon* and show them that the debt had been paid in full.

Now that you understand the analogy, allow yourself to feel it. There you are in prison for life. And believe me, the prisons back then were much worse than our modern prisons. But then, someone comes along and pays the debt in full, releasing you;

110

the debt is canceled. You are amazed but assume the worst. This must be some wealthy slave owner. He will make you his slave which will be worse than prison! But then you find out it was a relative who gave everything he had to pay your debt. He is now penniless and homeless, but he did that because he loved you that much. You are humbled and so appreciative; you have been set free. How could anyone love and value you that much?

Now, transfer this to spiritual truth. You are separated from God forever because of your sin. Hell is to become your eternal destination. That is what Paul is implying when he says, *you were dead in your sins.* Through the redemption of Jesus Christ, God *made you alive with Christ. He forgave us all our sins.* He accomplished this by canceling *the charge of our legal indebtedness (kerigraphon), which stood against us and condemned us; he has taken it away, nailing it to the cross.* Do you see the analogy? He took our *kerigraphon*, which contained the list of all our sins, removed it from our prison door, nailed it to his cross, and paid the penalty in full for our sin! It cost him everything. All the suffering and pain was for us, to set us free from sin and death. He then *disarmed the powers and authorities...made a public spectacle of them, triumphing over them by the cross.* He took away Satan's power to keep us from God. We are free once again to choose to have an intimate relationship with our heavenly Father. What a powerful analogy!

Now, let me share something equally as amazing. In John 19:30, the last word that Jesus spoke before he died was *tetelestai.* You may be familiar with the common English translation, *"It is finished."* What a picture. The *kerigraphon* had been nailed to the cross, and Jesus writes across it in big letters, by his blood, *the debt has been paid in full.* When I first heard this analogy, it broke my heart. Jesus did that for me. Yes, I understood this truth in the Bible, but the analogy helped me to feel it! The truth was able to sink deep into my heart and revolutionize how I saw the cross. I hope it does the same for you as well.

THE VALUE OF A PAINTING

Let me give you another analogy. What is the value of a painting? If we look at the physical materials, all paintings have pretty much the same value: the cost of the canvas and the cost of the paint spread across the canvas. If we look simply at the physical materials, most paintings would be valued at about fifty dollars, give or take. But of course, we know paintings are often valued at a much higher price.

What makes a painting valuable? The first thing is the artist. If the artist is famous, his paintings are highly valued. But the full extent of the value lies in how much someone is willing to pay for the painting. Today, paintings can sell for several hundred million dollars. That sounds outlandish to most of us, and we would call those paintings priceless.

Now, let us use the same reasoning when it comes to human beings. The physical materials that make up our body, in and of themselves, have very little value. You might well say, *"But the value of a human being lies in his intellect, skill, creativity, etc."* Yes, that is how people value each other, but still, we are all the same inside. We value the abilities of others, but who values us just because we exist? When we compare ourselves to the world, we are simply a microdot. When we compare the world to the universe, the world becomes the microdot. Honestly, what value do we have as people?

But when we recognize that we have been created by the greatest Creator in the universe, we start to have true value by our very existence. The Creator of the universe made us and sees us as highly valuable. We are not a microdot to Him, even though He encompasses the universe. And if that were not enough, when the Creator lost us due to our own choice – when we left Him and became separated from God – the Creator

Himself paid the highest price imaginable to buy us back again. That is the message of the Gospel. God came into this world, in the person of Jesus Christ, and sacrificed Himself on the cross to redeem us, or literally *buy us back* from the devil.

Here is the most amazing part, if there can be anything more amazing. When the Creator bought us back, unlike a painting, He did not take us against our will. Free will is still at the heart of God's nature. His redemption was for everyone, but we still have to choose to come back to Him. After that great sacrifice and His excruciating suffering on the cross, He simply offers us the ability or freedom to choose to come back to Him. Salvation is a gift that we must receive as I previously explained. When we fully understand this truth, how could we do anything but choose this wonderful gift? If that does not touch deeply into your very being, I cannot imagine what will. He did this not because of our talents or abilities, but simply because we came into existence, and He considers us His children. I am valued because I am!

A BOY AND HIS BOAT

There is much power in storytelling. I first heard this final analogy when I was a young boy, but I have never forgotten it. It has always been in the back of my mind, helping shape my belief about the way God values me.

It is the story of a young boy who was very creative. He liked to make things. His favorite creation was a sailboat. He actually carved the boat out of wood, added a rudder and mast, and, finally, cut out and attached a cloth sail. It was so well made that it floated nicely in the river near his home. He loved lying on the shore, watching his little boat float along, gently guided by the wind. One lovely afternoon it was so peaceful that he fell asleep. When he awoke, he could not see his boat. He looked downstream and, far in the distance, saw a speck of white. He took off running as fast as he could. He ran, and ran, and ran, until he finally fell, exhausted. Then he started crying. He had lost his precious boat.

Over the next couple of weeks, he could not get out of his funk. He was depressed and discouraged. Nothing could lift his spirits, and he felt like life was no longer worth living. Then one afternoon he was walking through town and happened to glance in a shop window. There was his boat! He had no doubt. He ran into the shop and was so excited he could hardly speak. "Sir, that's my boat."

"What are you talking about?" the shopkeeper asked.

"That boat in your window, that's my boat. I made it."

The shopkeeper shook his head, "I don't know if you made it or not. All I know is that someone brought it to me, and I bought it from him. It is now my boat, and if you want it, you will have to buy it from me."

Without hesitating, he turned and left the shop and ran home as fast as he could. He had been saving his money for a long time in order to buy a new bicycle. He had really been looking forward to that, but he did not even hesitate or think twice. He broke open his piggy bank, took all the money, ran back to that shopkeeper, dumped the money on the table and said, "Here's your money. I want my boat!"

As he walked out of the shop that day, he proudly held his little boat in his hands and said, "Now, you are doubly valuable to me. First, I made you, and when I lost you, I bought you back again."

Perhaps God has felt far away. *"Why would He think about me? Who am I?"* But now you know that you are <u>doubly</u> valuable to God. You are precious to God. Never forget that. Let it sink deep into your heart.

PERSONALIZING THE SCRIPTURE

Let us look once again at taking a verse and personalizing it so that we can "hear" God speaking this truth into our subconscious every day. We will use a verse already mentioned, Mathew 6:26:

> *Look at the birds of the air; they do not sow or reap or store away in barns, and yet your heavenly Father feeds them. Are you not much more valuable than they?*

> Here is a suggested paraphrase: *Dave, the animals are special to me. I made them and take care of them. But you are my dear son, and I am your Father. You are much more valuable to me than the animals.*

I am sure you also can find some good scriptures which communicate how much God values you. Find the verses you like best and personalize them. That is an excellent way to get this truth into your subconscious: I am valued unconditionally by God!

CHAPTER 9

NEED NUMBER THREE
THE NEED TO BE ACCEPTED

THE UNHEALTHY BELIEF:
I AM UNACCEPTABLE

SYMPTOMS OF THE BELIEF

- Feeling that others would not want to be friends with me
- Deflecting compliments
- Reacting to criticism defensively
- Needing reassurance from others
- Expecting rejection from others
- Feeling shame or guilt frequently
- Being a people pleaser
- Putting myself down frequently
- Being overly harsh on myself
- Struggling to forgive myself

We have a deep inner need to be accepted, but it is quite common to feel that I am not quite good enough for others. Therefore, it is hard to feel accepted. We learn that we have to pass certain behavioral expectations to be accepted by others. The problem is, we might meet the expectations of one group and be accepted but fail the expectations of another and feel rejected. This is quite common for teenagers. Parents have certain behavioral guidelines, but peers have other expectations. You want to be accepted by your friends, but then you come into disfavor with your parents. It can be quite confusing, and we often focus on the disfavor or rejection, letting that shape our self-image.

From these experiences, there is another unhealthy belief which can develop: I must be good or perfect in order to be accepted. This belief may cause us to go in one of two directions: Either perfectionism or feeling like a failure, which are two sides of the same coin.

We will begin with perfectionism. We have all met people who are very hard on themselves and who have to be the best at everything they do. They are also very hard on others, often looking with disdain on those who fail to meet their high expectations. They have a strong need to be accepted and feel that their good behavior is bringing them acceptance. And, if others are not as good as they are, that only increases their acceptability.

They tend to build friendships around others with similar expectations, but those friendships are often superficial. Even though I feel I am performing well outwardly, I am not so confident inwardly. I do not want anyone to dig too deep, for they may discover that I am not as perfect as I project, and that would be unacceptable. Ultimately, to stay on this side of the coin involves a tight box of rules and regulations and a lot of denial. Does this remind you of our discussion about the Pharisees when we looked at the Pharisee and the tax collector?

The other side of the coin is the person who simply feels like a failure. He also believes that *"I must be good or perfect in order to be accepted,"* but feels that he can never measure up. He begins to expect rejection and accepts the fact that he is unacceptable. He may even become good at being bad because then he may feel accepted by others that are seen as unacceptable.

Many people are somewhere between these two extremes but still struggle with not feeling good enough. Their deep need to feel accepted goes unmet, and there is a certain emptiness inside.

Sadly, many people have the same belief about God. I must be good or perfect in order to be accepted by God. I see God as the judge, and if I perform well enough, He will love and accept me. If I think I am good enough, I will tend to become like the Pharisees of the New Testament: perfectionistic and judgmental. If I feel that I cannot measure up to God's standard, I will most likely turn away from God, saying, "If God does not want to have anything to do with me, I do not want to have anything to do with Him." Both sides of the coin come from the same belief. The problem is that we have the wrong belief about God.

THE HEALTHY BELIEF:
I AM IMPERFECT BUT STILL
ACCEPTABLE AND FORGIVABLE

It is actually good to see myself as imperfect and sinful because that is reality. Deep down inside I already know that, but I still want to be accepted. When I start with the understanding that I am not perfect, that takes away a lot of pressure and eradicates the need for denial. The Apostle John said it well in I John 1:8-9, *"If we claim to be without sin, we deceive ourselves and the truth is not in us. If we confess our sins, he is faithful and just and will forgive us our sins and purify us from all unrighteousness."*

With God, acceptance and forgiveness are intimately tied together. I may be imperfect but discover that I am still acceptable and forgivable. When we accept the gift of salvation by confessing our sin and inviting Him to be a part of our lives, He forgives us and takes away the sin that separates us from God.

People judge us by our behavior, but God is much different. God's acceptance starts with His unconditional love for us. Yes, sin separates us from God, but that is why He had Plan B. He accepts us unconditionally as a Father and forgives us unconditionally through the cross of Jesus Christ. The Apostle Paul said it this way, *"But God demonstrates his own love for us in this: While we were still sinners, Christ died for us"* (Romans 5:8). We did not have to be good enough for Christ to die for us. He showed His love by sacrificing His life for us while we were still separated from Him. How wonderful is that!

GETTING THIS TRUTH INTO
THE SUBCONSCIOUS MIND

To show that the God of the Old Testament is the same God Whom we see in the New Testament, I would like to give you three wonderful Old Testament passages which reveal God's unconditional acceptance and forgiveness.

ISAIAH 49:14-15

*14 But Zion said, "The LORD has forsaken me,
the Lord has forgotten me."
15 "Can a mother forget the baby at her breast
and have no compassion on the child she has borne?*

Though she may forget, I will not forget you!

Zion is Israel, God's chosen people in the Old Testament. They were going through a very difficult time and felt that God had forsaken them. They even felt that God had forgotten all about them. Perhaps you have felt that way.

God spoke through the prophet and asked them a question, *"Can a mother forget the baby at her breast?"* This question implies that a mother can reject her nursing baby. What is your gut reaction to that question? *"No! A mother could never forget (reject) her baby."* That is the most powerful bond we know on earth.

But God answers His own question, *"Yes, she may reject her nursing baby."* We all know this to be true. We never understand it, but we have seen, in this fallen world, that a mother can reject her newborn baby. Some babies have been left on the doorsteps of a church; even worse, some have been left abandoned on the side of the road. We are horrified when it happens, we can hardly believe it, but yes, it does happen.

Then God emphatically makes this declaration: *"I WILL NEVER FORGET YOU!"* We are His children, forever in His heart. His heart breaks when we are separated from Him, and His heart rejoices when we come to Him and accept the gift of His salvation. Yes, if we never receive that gift, we will ultimately be eternally separated from God, but that is not God's will. II Peter 3:9 says, *"The Lord is not slow in keeping his promise, as some understand slowness. Instead he is patient with you, not wanting anyone to perish, but everyone to come to repentance."* If we do not come to repentance, it is our choice, not God's.

PSALM 103:12

As far as the east is from the west,
so far has he removed our transgressions from us.

121

What an amazing verse! It reminds us that God actually removed the sin from us and placed it upon Jesus as He sacrificed His life on the cross. The Jews experienced forgiveness through the sacrifice of the lamb on the Day of Atonement each year. The lamb pointed toward the sacrifice of the Messiah who was to come. Here God tells us how far God has removed our sin: *as far as the east is from the west.* This line does not follow the circumference of the earth, thank God, or it would eventually come back to us. No, this line is straight. Our sin is at one end of this line, we are at the other end, and both ends have no end! This verse declares that God has removed our sin an infinite distance from us. It is forever gone – how freeing. I am imperfect but still acceptable and forgivable.

ZEPHANIAH 3:17

The Lord your God is with you,
the Mighty Warrior who saves.
He will take great delight in you;
in his love he will no longer rebuke you,
but will rejoice over you with singing.

Just when you thought it could not get any better than the last verse, look closely at this one. God is always with us. Hebrews 13:5 makes the same declaration, *"Never will I (Jesus) leave you; never will I forsake you."* Here in Zephaniah, Jesus is *the Mighty Warrior who saves.* It took great strength and infinite love to willingly go through that much suffering for us.

God *takes great delight in us and rejoices over us with singing.* In this last verse, I think of a mother rocking her newborn baby. You can see the delight in her eyes as she softly sings a lullaby to her baby, gently lulling him to peaceful sleep, her heart full of intense joy. That is God, our wonderful Father.

Let these verses sink deep into your subconscious as you personalize them and allow God to speak them into your heart every day. I am imperfect but still acceptable and forgivable! Thank you, Father.

THE IMPORTANCE OF ACCEPTING AND FORGIVING OURSELVES

Now that we have seen how God accepts and forgives us, it is important to take the next step: Accept and forgive yourself. This can sometimes be the hardest part. I have heard many people say, "I know God forgives me, but I just can't forgive myself." The deeper God's truth sinks into our subconscious, the easier it is to begin accepting and forgiving ourselves; however, we may need to consciously recognize how important this is and give ourselves permission to accept and forgive ourselves.

While at seminary, I was talking to a fellow student, and he said something I will never forget:

"All my life I was fat. I tried every diet in the book, but nothing worked. I might lose a little, but I would quickly gain it right back. It finally dawned on me that I was rejecting myself for being fat. Then I realized that in doing so, I was rejecting the God who made me. So, I changed my thinking. I started focusing on all the positive things in my life instead of simply focusing on my weight. I began to like myself again. And you know what? After that, I began consistently losing weight!"

I knew that what I had just heard was important. In the years since that time, I have thought a great deal about the psychological dynamics of what he said. Many times we struggle with accepting ourselves. We think, *"I must not accept myself as I am because then I won't change."* But it is

123

possible that we may actually be rejecting ourselves and sabotaging our ability to change (that may need a little time to sink in).

My friend started to understand that he had been sabotaging his own weight loss. When we do not accept ourselves, we fear that others will not accept us. I muse, *"They don't accept me because I am fat"* (or whatever I am telling myself about why others do not accept me). Sadly, I am afraid to lose the weight or change in some other way because others still may not accept me, and then what will be my excuse? That would be more depressing. The belief that *I am unacceptable* is keeping me from growing and changing.

Here is a key truth. When I speak of self-acceptance, I am not talking about accepting my behavior, or appearance, or any outward criteria. I am talking about accepting myself as a person, loved and accepted by God, and capable of change and growth.

I had to learn how to accept myself and be a friend to myself. When I was in high school, I would make some small mistake – or do something I thought was dumb – and get frustrated with myself and be depressed for days. Something happened in college that helped me understand why that was happening.

One particular morning, I did something that had me quite upset. I have no idea what it was, but I remember well what happened that evening in my dorm room. I was standing in front of a La-Z-Boy chair in our room, and my roommate was doing something at his desk. I was still mad at myself for what had happened that morning and started cutting myself down – out loud. I cannot remember what I said, but I can imagine it was something like this, "I am so stupid. I can't do anything right." All of a sudden, my roommate rose up, and using both hands, grabbed my shoulders and shoved me down into that chair. He then stuck his index finger right up to my nose and shouted, "DON'T YOU EVER TALK ABOUT MY FRIEND LIKE THAT AGAIN!" Believe me, he was shouting and the spit was flying. After a few seconds, he started laughing, and I laughed; but afterward, I did some deep thinking.

The shock of that event penetrated a lot of defenses. The anger he expressed, and the fact that he said it in the third person as if I had been saying that about someone else, made me think. I would not have been saying that about someone else; I knew I was not that rude. But then, why was I saying that about myself? If someone else had been saying those words to me, I would be depressed, but when I say them to myself, I get depressed as well. I now understood why I would get so down in high school over some silly mistake. I had no grace for myself. Therefore, I had to learn how to be a friend to myself.

I started thinking about how I would treat a good friend if he were getting down on himself. I would encourage him and try to lift him up in some way. So, I started doing that to myself.

I began listening to those subconscious negative messages instead of just accepting them. Then, I would gently start encouraging myself, giving myself some grace, no longer being so hard on myself. As the months passed, I began to handle mistakes differently. I found myself examining the mistake and seeing how I could do better the next time. I was no longer cutting myself down. The subconscious belief was changing, and I was treating myself differently. I liked the change. In fact, I started thinking, *"Who says I have to be so hard on myself? I am the only person I'm stuck with twenty-four hours a day. I can get away from everyone else, at least for a while, but I can't get away from myself. If I don't treat myself very well, that can make for a miserable life."*

Furthermore, I discovered that in accepting myself and giving myself some grace, I was changing and growing more than ever. When I would get down on myself and be depressed for days, I was just dwelling on how bad I was. But now, as I started examining my mistakes and learning from them so I

125

could do better next time, I was actually growing and changing through my mistakes! As I let God's acceptance and forgiveness sink in, I was able to accept and forgive myself. I was now on a journey of growth, and it felt great!

THE POWER TO LIVE A HOLY LIFE

We just looked at how God's unconditional acceptance can help us accept ourselves and live more disciplined lives. But did you know it can also help you discover the power to overcome sin? This is important because we all have areas of weakness and struggle with thoughts and behaviors that the Bible describes as sin. We may feel guilty, but we start to believe that we cannot overcome these besetting sins.

Guilt is a very important emotion. God has given us a conscience that helps move us away from sin. When we do something the Bible says is wrong, it is good and natural to feel guilty. This leads us to repentance, which is agreeing with God that the behavior is wrong and seeking to turn from it. But if we continue the behavior, our conscience is weakened, and we may give up trying to change.

If we give up our struggle to overcome sin, it can lead to a very wrong interpretation of God's unconditional acceptance and forgiveness. In order to reduce guilt, I may try to justify my behavior. The thought might be something like this, *"If God forgives me unconditionally, does it matter that I continue a wrong behavior? I will live in God's grace and mercy."*

The Apostle Paul had to deal with this same issue in his day. He encountered God on the road to Damascus in Acts 9 and changed from being a legalistic Pharisee to being a Christian filled with the love and forgiveness of God. It revolutionized his life, and he went all over Asia Minor sharing the Good News of God's saving grace. But there were those who used that grace as an excuse to continue in sin. We read about Paul's answer to this problem in Romans 5:18 – 6:4:

126

18Just as one trespass resulted in condemnation for all people, so also one righteous act resulted in justification and life for all people. 19 For just as through the disobedience of the one man the many were made sinners, so also through the obedience of the one man the many will be made righteous.

20 The law was brought in so that the trespass might increase. But where sin increased, grace increased all the more, 21 so that, just as sin reigned in death, so also grace might reign through righteousness to bring eternal life through Jesus Christ our Lord.

6:1 What shall we say, then? Shall we go on sinning so that grace may increase? 2 By no means! We are those who have died to sin; how can we live in it any longer? 3 Or don't you know that all of us who were baptized into Christ Jesus were baptized into his death? 4 We were therefore buried with him through baptism into death in order that, just as Christ was raised from the dead through the glory of the Father, we too may live a new life.

Verse 18 is speaking of the sin of Adam which brought death (separation from God) to all people, and the righteous act (sacrificial death) of Jesus Christ which brought justification (forgiveness of sin) for all people. Verse 20 lets us know that even when there is great sin, God's grace covers that sin. This is wonderful news for all of us. We can never be so bad that God's grace cannot bring about forgiveness. I have known many people who felt they were too sinful to come to God. That simply is not true. God loves you and wants you to receive Jesus as your Savior so that you can experience the gift of forgiveness.

But in chapter 6, Paul switches gears and is talking to those who have received God's grace but have chosen to continue their sinful behavior thinking, *"It's OK. God's grace will cover that."* To answer, Paul uses the strongest negative in the Greek language, which is translated in the New International Version, "By no means!" It can literally be translated, "No! Never!" and the King James Version says, "God forbid!" The purpose of the cross and God's wonderful grace and forgiveness are to set us free from sin, not to overlook or disregard our sin. Sin hurts us. Why would we want to continue to hurt ourselves?

In fact, this is an important truth to get into our subconscious. Sin is that which hurts me and hurts others. When I came to believe this key truth about sin, it revolutionized my relationship with God. As a teenager, I struggled with sin, and it hurt my relationship with God. We tend to think in rational constructs. The following was a rational construct which plagued me, *"God hates sin. I am a sinner; therefore..."* That construct led me to think, *"...God must hate me."* But I had been taught for years that God loved me. How do I reconcile that? I felt so weak against the power of sin.

As I began to get the truth of God's love into my subconscious, my logical construct began to change. I started to understand that sin was an evil force within me, but it was not me. Romans 7:14-24 helped me understand this important truth (we will be looking more fully at this passage later on). The Apostle Paul was sharing his testimony, describing sin as an evil force within him causing him to do the things he did not want to do and not do the things he wanted to do.

The truth that sin is that which hurts me and others enabled me to build a new rational construct. I started realizing, *"God hates sin because He loves me so much."* That made sense; I could relate to that. If I love someone deeply, and something is hurting the one I love, I hate that which is hurting them. For the first time, I was able to hate the sin within me while still liking myself. I was able to accept myself as God's beloved child. My desire to win the struggle over sin became much more intense. A power rose up inside that I had not previously known. I was becoming an *overcomer*. I John 5:4-5 proclaims this truth very well:

> *⁴ Everyone born of God overcomes the world. This is the victory that has overcome the world, even our faith. ⁵ Who is it that overcomes the world? Only the one who believes that Jesus is the Son of God.*

If that were not enough, we have something far greater than increased willpower and self-control to draw upon when we commit our lives to Jesus Christ. The Bible says that we also receive the power of the Holy Spirit. God Himself comes to live within us through His Spirit.

> *¹⁶ And I (Jesus) will ask the Father, and he will give you another advocate to help you and be with you forever— ¹⁷ the Spirit of truth. The world cannot accept him, because it neither sees him nor knows him. But you know him, for he lives with you and will be in you* (John 14:16-17).

> *But you will receive power when the Holy Spirit comes on you; and you will be my witnesses in Jerusalem, and in all Judea and Samaria, and to the ends of the earth* (Acts 1:8).

One of the reasons Alcoholics Anonymous worked well as one of the best support groups to help people overcome addiction was step two of the twelve steps. It recognized that we need God's power to ultimately overcome addiction. Many people have found that when they do not simply rely on their own willpower but also draw upon the power of the Holy Spirit within them, they can and do overcome sin.

129

I would like to share one more key to overcoming sin. This will also lead us perfectly into our discussion of esteem need number four. I mentioned earlier that much of our sin grows out of our hurts and unmet needs. When we are able to get the truth of God's unconditional love, worth, acceptance, and forgiveness into our subconscious, many of our deepest hurts begin to heal and our deepest needs start to be met. You are guessing correctly if you are thinking, *"If sin grows out of our hurts and unmet needs, then perhaps righteousness grows out of God meeting those needs."* That is exactly what I saw happening in my own life during my college years.

We will now look at need number four and hopefully develop a whole new way of understanding our attractiveness.

CHAPTER 10

NEED NUMBER FOUR
THE NEED TO BE ATTRACTIVE

At this point, some of you may be saying, "Wait a minute! Didn't you say we were not going to deal with ego issues in this book?" What makes you think this is an ego issue? "Well, physical attractiveness, that's an ego issue, right?" Who said I was talking about *physical* attractiveness? The truth is, if we understand this need correctly, it is an esteem need, not an ego need. But unfortunately, most of us have bought into one of the biggest lies our society has placed upon us: Our attractiveness is based on our physical appearance. This lie has done more to damage our self-image than anything else. If I can properly debunk this lie, it may revolutionize how you see yourself!

THE UNHEALTHY BELIEF:
I AM UNATTRACTIVE
(FOCUSING ON PHYSICAL APPEARANCE)

If we were to take a survey of how many people are satisfied with their physical appearance, what percentage of respondents do you think would answer in the affirmative? Most of us have aspects of our appearance that we do not like, and we try various ways to make ourselves more physically attractive. Women spend millions of dollars each year on cosmetics. Men pump iron and use steroids to bulk up muscles. Cosmetic surgeons are wealthy because of this unhealthy belief. But often, it does not matter what we do; we still do not like how we look. Not only that, we make the assumption that others will not like us as well. We think our attractiveness to others lies in our appearance. We feel helpless because there is really very little we can do to change our physical appearance.

As a junior high student, I did not like the way I looked and felt I had some very good reasons. My first pair of glasses came when I was six, and each year my prescription increased. At thirteen, my glasses had nice thick lenses, and glasses were not as fashionable as today. Four-eyes was a common nickname for those who wore glasses.

I was also convinced the frames caused my ears to stick out. When I looked in the mirror, I saw Mickey Mouse (we tend to exaggerate the areas we do not like). In the mid-sixties, the Beatles were very popular. They were known for having *long* hair, although at that point in their career they had more of a bowl haircut with the hair simply covering their ears. I was stuck with short hair because that was popular in the fifties, and my parents thought long hair was inappropriate for boys. I begged my parents to let my hair grow longer, but they refused. All I wanted was to grow my hair over my ears to make them less noticeable. Of course, I never had the courage to say that to my parents. (Although it probably would not have made a difference in their decision.)

If that were not bad enough, my face was covered with acne. Those red spots glared back at me every time I looked in the mirror. The main acne treatment at that time was Clearasil which came in clear or brown versions. You can probably guess, I used the brown. I had to cover those red pimples. I realize now that the brown smeared across my face probably looked worse than the pimples themselves.

At fifteen, my parents allowed me to get contact lens. I was so grateful to finally be rid of those ugly glasses. The acne began to clear up as I started high school, and I was even allowed to grow my hair a little longer during my junior year. As I look back at my senior pictures, I can see that I was a fairly handsome young man. But back then, I still did not like the way I looked. When we look in the mirror, our negative self-image will often distort how we see ourselves.

Many years ago, I was counseling with an attractive twenty-one-year-old female. She said during one session, "When I was younger, I was fat. I now realize that I am no longer fat, but when I look in the mirror, I still see myself as fat and don't like the way I look." The subconscious definitely distorts our perceptions.

Unfortunately, this is all too common. We find aspects of our physical appearance that we do not like, and that becomes the center of our focus. It is especially troublesome during the teen and young adult years when we desire to be attractive to the opposite sex. That negative focus robs us of confidence and can curtail our ability to build good, healthy friendships. All because we believe that we are not attractive to others! We have bought into society's greatest lie.

With that said, let me ask you a question to change your focus: What attracts you to another person as a friend? What makes you think to yourself, *"I like that person, I enjoy being around them?"* Think about your answer for a few minutes before you read on.

I have asked this question to hundreds of people over the last three decades. There have been a variety of answers: openness, friendliness, honesty, sense of humor, kindness, thoughtfulness, a smile, to name a few. But strangely, there is one answer I rarely, if ever, hear: "What attracts me to another person as a friend is their physical appearance." As you thought about your answer, I will wager that it was not one of your answers either. We realize appearance is not what causes us to be attracted to another person, but when we think about other people being attracted to us, we often focus on our appearance.

Yes, physical appearance does play a part, especially initially. But ultimately, we will decide if we like a person based on the way they treat us, not on how they look. And if that is not true for you, I am sorry to say, you are pretty shallow. (I am just being truthful.) I have just given you the secret to the healthy belief that is needed to meet this esteem need.

THE HEALTHY BELIEF: MY ATTRACTIVENESS IS BASED IN MY PERSONALITY

All the many answers I receive when I ask, "What attracts you to another person?" describe the personality. Personality is the combination of traits and behaviors that make up our character. Personality includes the way I treat others. Unfortunately, personality is usually subconsciously driven. If I have a low self-image, it will tend to negatively affect how I relate to others. If there are aspects I do not like about myself, it becomes difficult to relax and enjoy relationships. That puts a negative bent on my personality and makes me less attractive, but I will tend to blame the areas of myself I do not like, such as my appearance.

Here is the good news: I can change the way I treat others. If my personality changes in a positive way, others will be more attracted to me as a friend. Utilizing the model for the mind can help me become much more proactive in my behavior. I can gain insight into the way I treat others and form good goals for treating others better and for relaxing and being

134

friendlier. I saw that happening in my own life during my college years.

More than that, my personality can even affect how people view me physically. That truth hit me squarely in the face when I was working with Youth for Christ in the mid-seventies. I was the Campus Life Staff Director of two towns in northwest Ohio, my alma mater and the town next door. Each spring, Youth for Christ would host a fundraising banquet to raise money for the coming year. We would try to get a well-known speaker who would draw a large crowd as we encouraged people to give generously.

This particular year, our speaker was Merrill Womach, a businessman, pilot, and gospel artist from Oregon. He was involved in a plane wreck in 1961 that left him disfigured with third-degree burns on his hands, legs, and all over his head. Mel White, biographer and film producer, wrote a book and produced a film documentary of Merrill's accident and subsequent recovery.

Since Merrill Womach was not well known in our area, we obtained the film documentary to show in churches all over northwest Ohio where Youth for Christ was in the area high schools. I showed the film in about ten churches covering the two school districts I oversaw.

As the film opens, you see Merrill Womach in the distance, with his back to the camera, describing that fateful morning when he ascended from the county airport in Beaver Marsh, Oregon, in his Cessna. He loved to fly. As he continued talking, the camera was slowly moving closer and closer. He dramatically described how the engine on that single-engine Cessna sputtered and failed. He did a U-turn, trying to make it back to the airport, but had neither the height nor speed to cover the distance and crashed into the wooded area where he was now standing. The plane caught fire immediately, but fortunately, he was still conscious and able to crawl out of the wreckage, but not before being severely burned. If he had not been wearing a fireproof leather jacket, he most likely would have died.

At this point in his story, the camera was about five feet from him, and for the first time, he turns around so you can see his face. As you have probably seen other burn victims, you can picture the scene. Even though he had many surgeries and skin grafts, the scars were quite noticeable. I remember my initial gut reaction as the camera centered on his face. I have no doubt that Mel White purposely hid Merrill Womach's face to bring about that response. But during the rest of the film, you get to know Merrill. You meet his family, walk through his recovery, learn of his many struggles, and hear him sing.

At one point in the film, his wife talks about the aftermath of the accident. She said, "Before the accident, Merrill was a very handsome man." They flashed a picture of him before the accident. Then she shared her reaction at the hospital when she first saw him, his head all charred and swollen (another quick picture, this time in the hospital). She wondered if she would ever be attracted to him again. But she closed by saying, "…but now, I see him as handsome as ever, and love him more than ever."

I firmly believe that she was telling the truth. How do I know that? From my own experience. As I said, I watched the film about ten times, and then finally was able to meet him as he came to the banquet and shared his story and sang for us. As I sat there enjoying his performance, I realized something. I was no longer noticing his scars. Instead, I was seeing his smile, enjoying his music, and marveling at the great peace and joy that radiated from this man. He looked very different to me from when he first turned toward the camera. His personality was changing how I saw him.

I would guess you have had similar experiences with people you have gotten to know. You may also relate to something else. Have you ever met someone you thought was very attractive at first, but when you got to know him, you did not find him that attractive at all? I will wager you have.

Is this all making sense to you? I hope so. I know society has brainwashed us quite effectively through the media, movies, commercials, etc. We are convinced that people are attracted to physical appearance, and I look nothing like those people I see on television or the big screen. Sadly, much of that is not even real. Magazines airbrush the models, and movie stars have hours of makeup added before they appear in front of the camera. I know a man who once owned a movie theater. He often met movie stars who were promoting the movies that were appearing on his screens. He said to me one day, "Those movie stars are not nearly as attractive in person as they are on the big screen." It was a shocking revelation to him.

To change that unhealthy belief, you need to be totally honest with yourself about how you see others, deep down inside, and then realize the same thing is true about how others see you. Others are not focusing on your appearance, they are noticing how you treat them. They are getting to know you through your personality.

THE REAL NEED:
SHARING THE LOVE OF JESUS

I have tried my best to convince you that your attractiveness is based on your personality, but with all that said, this is not the true esteem need. Deep down inside, my greatest sense of fulfillment is when I feel that I have positively influenced another person. My deepest need is to feel purpose and usefulness, to be of value to others. When I feel that others are attracted to me because of what I give to them rather than what I take from them, I experience an inner fullness.

Once again, God is the only one that can truly meet this deepest need. Allow me to take the first three esteem needs

137

and apply them to this fourth need. God desires to fill me with his love, worth, acceptance, and forgiveness to meet my deepest needs. But then, out of that fullness, I discover that I begin to love, value, accept and forgive others as that fullness begins to flow from me to others. I begin meeting the deepest needs of others as my deepest needs are constantly being met by God. I am becoming more attractive to others through my compassion, acceptance, and love (very attractive personality traits). But I am discovering that others are not being attracted to me, but to the love of Jesus Christ within me. Instead of creating arrogance, it is building a deep humility. I do not deserve any of this, but God is graciously transforming my life through His love. I am becoming more like Jesus Christ. With this said, let me rephrase this forth esteem need, so it reflects our true need: The need to reflect the love, compassion, and forgiveness of Jesus toward others.

Do you remember what Jesus said to the woman at the well? *"The water I give them will become in them a spring of water welling up to eternal life."* He was comparing his love, which he described as living water, to an artesian well. In an artesian well, there is so much water that it pushes through the hole in the ground and continually overflows. When we are able to get the truth of God's unconditional love into our subconscious and are being replenished by that love daily, it not only fills our lives but begins to flow from us to others.

One of the most fascinating Messianic prophecies in the Old Testament is found in Isaiah 53. It is often entitled "The Suffering Servant." This passage communicates in detail the sacrificial suffering and death of the Messiah. It also discusses the atoning aspect of the crucifixion in stating that he bore the sins of the world on his own body. And it was written over seven hundred years before the Messiah, Jesus Christ, was born. It is truly an amazing passage, and I encourage you to read it, but I have not included it here as my purpose is to point out only one verse at this time. Isaiah 53:2 says, *"He had no beauty or majesty to attract us to him, nothing in his appearance that we should desire him."* In speaking of the Messiah, Isaiah says that he was not handsome. In fact, there was nothing in his appearance which was attractive.

I firmly believe that Jesus was not very attractive. That goes along with the humble nature of the Messiah. After all, he was born in a barn and his bed was a cattle feeding trough. God does not seek spectacle and splendor. He values simplicity. One good example was King David. He was living in a great palace while God was living in a tent (the tabernacle). He felt guilty, so he wanted to build God a spectacular temple made of the finest cedar. God firmly let Nathan the prophet know that He was happy in the tent that He had resided in for the previous four hundred years.

> *7:1 After the king was settled in his palace and the LORD had given him rest from all his enemies around him, 2 he said to Nathan the prophet, "Here I am, living in a house of cedar, while the ark of God remains in a tent."*
>
> *3 Nathan replied to the king, "Whatever you have in mind, go ahead and do it, for the LORD is with you."*
>
> *4 But that night the word of the LORD came to Nathan, saying:*
>
> *5 "Go and tell my servant David, 'This is what the LORD says: Are you the one to build me a house to dwell in? 6 I have not dwelt in a house from the day I brought the Israelites up out of Egypt to this day. I have been moving from place to place with a tent as my dwelling. 7 Wherever I have moved with all the Israelites, did I ever say to any of their rulers whom I commanded to shepherd my people Israel, "Why have you not built me a house of cedar?"'* (I Samuel 7:1-7).

God loves humility because He Himself is humble. There was nothing in the appearance of Jesus that would attract people to him, but he was one of the most attractive men who ever lived. People were attracted to him by the thousands. They were attracted to his compassion, love, mercy, wisdom, etc. People everywhere were touched by the life of Christ, and He changed them and made them better people. Would you like to touch the lives of others the way Jesus did?

GOD'S GOAL FOR US

God's goal for us is that we affect the lives of others in a positive way as Jesus did. We see this in Romans 8:29, *"For those God foreknew he also predestined to be conformed to the image of his Son, that he might be the firstborn among many brothers and sisters."*

There are some big theological words in this verse which theologians have written books trying to explain, but allow me to attempt a simple paraphrase. "From the beginning, God knew us and had a plan for us. His goal was that we should become like Jesus Christ."

Let me illustrate this with a common human analogy. How many of you have known a couple who have been happily married for more than fifty years? Did you notice similarities in them? It is often said, "They are so perfect for each other; they even look alike!" Believe me, fifty years earlier, they were probably as different as any married couple can be. We often marry our opposite. But as we daily dwell together in a loving, intimate relationship, we slowly adapt to each other. Our mannerisms, habits, and other traits slowly rub off on each other. Our personalities begin to merge, and as people observe us, we seem to look alike. Once again, our personality affects our appearance.

This is what God desires to happen in our relationship with Christ. Although, Christ does not adapt to us; we adapt to him.

140

As we experience his love, compassion, acceptance, and forgiveness through an intimate relationship, these qualities begin to rub off on us. If we are constantly being filled by Christ, we are able to give to others. Even when we are not receiving much from others, we are still full. Christ is our source.

It is like Lake Hollywood, which provides water for the entire city of Hollywood and never runs dry. The reason it can continually provide water for such a large city is that it is continually being replenished by water flowing from the Santa Monica Mountains. The lake receives the water running down from the mountain range and is able to contain it because of the huge Mulholland Dam. The water is then redistributed to all the families living in Hollywood. Christ desires to be our source, and His love is so great that we cannot contain it. We can allow it to simply flow from us to others, and we are blessed in the giving.

We have looked at God's goal for us, but our goal is a little bit different. The Apostle Paul reveals our goal in Philippians 3:7-8:

> *But whatever were gains to me I now consider loss for the sake of Christ. What is more, I consider everything a loss because of the surpassing worth of knowing Christ Jesus my Lord, for whose sake I have lost all things. I consider them garbage, that I may gain Christ.*

For the context of these two verses, we need to go to Philippians 3:1-6. There, we see that Paul was talking about Christians who were acting confident or arrogant because they were convinced that God loved them because they were so good. He described it as *confidence in the flesh*. He let them know – if anyone thought they had confidence in the flesh – that he had more. He went on to brag a little about all his accomplishments as a well-respected Pharisee. At one time, he had believed God loved him because he was so good.

But then he met Christ on the road to Damascus. He was confronted with the unconditional love of Christ and realized that all his righteous deeds amounted to nothing in God's eyes. Those behaviors which he had thought were gaining him God's favor he now considered loss for the sake of Christ. In fact, he considered everything loss except the surpassing value of *knowing Christ Jesus*. In comparison, he considered everything else *garbage*. The King James Version uses more colorful language by literally translating the word as *dung,* better known to us as cow manure. Get the picture?

That married couple did not set out to become like each other fifty years ago. They simply began to build a loving, caring relationship. As each day, week, month, and year went by, their love and intimacy grew. As they dwelt together in a safe, loving environment, their subconscious beliefs shifted toward what they were experiencing from each other. Without even trying, they adapted to each other, and their personalities began to merge in a beautiful way. That relationship which the Bible describes as two people becoming one can actually happen in our personalities.

For decades, the Apostle Paul had tried to be a good Jew. But he was only changing the outside while God desired change on the inside, in his heart. His focus began to shift. Now, his goal was simply to know Christ Jesus, to spend time with Christ each day, to soak up the love and acceptance which enabled him to love and accept others. He went from being a judgmental, legalistic Pharisee to being a loving Christian who reflected the compassion of Christ.

Allow that to become your main goal, your key focus: To walk with Christ daily in an intimate relationship, reading the Bible and communing with God in prayer. Allow Him to communicate His love, compassion, acceptance, and forgiveness through His Word and through His Spirit. Allow the truth of God's Word to penetrate deeply. Allow your subconscious to experience this truth and be *transformed by the renewing of your mind*. If you do this, God's goal will happen automatically as you progressively become more like Jesus Christ. His personality will rub off on you, and He will use you to touch the lives of many people, just like Christ.

CHAPTER 11

NEED NUMBER FIVE
THE NEED TO CHANGE AND GROW

THE UNHEALTHY BELIEF:
I AM UNCHANGEABLE

SYMPTOMS OF THE BELIEF

- Believing you cannot change
- Feeling stuck in a rut
- Trying to hide aspects of your personality from others
- Getting defensive when someone gives you constructive criticism
- Deflecting compliments
- Avoiding new tasks or challenges
- Fearing failure

By the time we reach adulthood, many of us have become convinced that we cannot change. We looked at some of the reasons for that in the model for the mind. Without insight or understanding, the conscious mind goes along with whatever the subconscious tells us is true about ourselves. We live in our comfort zone, and the defenses protect unhealthy beliefs, which drive unhealthy behavior. We would like to change, but we believe we cannot. We feel stuck. Society even has a nice little phrase to help us feel better about not being able to change: You can't teach an old dog new tricks.

One of the sad aspects of this belief is that it helps lock in all of the other unhealthy beliefs. Why try to change if I cannot? I am afraid to approach new challenges for fear of failing. I tread on through life, year after year, with very little change. Life is dull and colorless because I have a need to grow, but that is not happening.

This described me quite well in high school. But in college, when I discovered I could change, my life began to blossom. I started to value constructive criticism. I looked forward to new tasks or challenges. It was not the end of the world if I failed. I simply learned from my mistakes and did better the next time. It felt like I moved from a black and white world to a world full of color.

THE HEALTHY BELIEF:
I AM A GROWING, CHANGING PERSON

As adults, we stop growing physically, but we need to keep growing mentally, socially, and spiritually. All too often, we stop growing in each of those areas.

First of all, we stop growing mentally. In school, we had to read many books. Most of those books were boring for us at the time, but we were made to read them to get a good grade. We were glad to get away from school and stopped reading. Our job may not have required any reading, so we determined it was unnecessary.

What we fail to realize is that now we have the freedom to read whatever we want to read. Good books can help us grow, and they can also be quite interesting. Self-help books are plentiful and cover many different topics. Even novels can help us grow as we experience life alongside the protagonist in the novel. The protagonist has various problems and struggles, but then, by the end of the book, gains the insight and understanding which helps change his life. Those same insights may help you change and grow as well.

Too often, we stop growing socially. In school, we may have had a variety of friends, but as we became adults, we lost touch with those friends and did not take the time to build new friendships. Relationships change from year-to-year, and building a friendship takes time and energy. If I already tend to feel that no one would want to be my friend, it is much easier to simply let friendships dwindle away. After all, rejection is just too painful.

Finally, we often do not grow spiritually either. I may have been very excited when I first accepted Christ into my life as Lord and Savior, but after a while, the newness of the message of the Gospel gets covered by the cares of life. Working, taking care of children, shopping, watching television, etc. takes up most of my day. I simply do not have the time to spend reading the Bible and talking to God. I still may go to church one day a week, but even that may drop off when I start going to the lake on weekends during the summer. I simply do not have time for God.

When I stop growing, my self-image becomes static. I continue to see myself as I did when I was five years old. And remember, I was not mature enough at that age to develop good, healthy, balanced opinions about who I am.

HOW GOD WANTS TO MEET THIS NEED

As we begin to examine how God wants to meet this esteem need, I want to refer back to a passage of scripture we looked at as we discussed the need to be loved unconditionally:

> *16 I pray that out of his glorious riches he may strengthen you with power through his Spirit in your inner being, 17 so that Christ may dwell in your hearts through faith. And I pray that you, being rooted and established in love, 18 may have power, together with all the Lord's holy people, to grasp how wide and long and high and deep is the love of Christ, 19 and to know this love that surpasses knowledge—that you may be filled to the measure of all the fullness of God. 20 Now to him who is able to do immeasurably more than all we ask or imagine, according to his power that is at work within us* (Ephesians 3:16-20).

The Apostle Paul prayed that the Ephesians would be able to experience both the power and the love of Christ. We first looked at receiving the love of Christ, but now I want to focus on the other part of the prayer. God wants us to experience His power through the Holy Spirit dwelling within us. We all have a degree of willpower in our lives, but we need to take advantage of the supernatural power of the Holy Spirit who comes to reside within us when we receive Christ as our Lord and Savior. When we recognize that God is living inside each of us, our ability to change and grow can increase exponentially.

You will notice that I added verse 20 to the passage above. *"[God] is able to do immeasurably more than all we ask or imagine, according to his power that is at work within us."* This verse coincides with verse 16 where Paul is speaking of the power of the Holy Spirit working within us. When we first read those words, we might think, "God is going to do great things **for** me. More than I could ever imagine." But that is not what the verse is saying. When Paul adds the words, *"according to His power that is at work within us,"* He is letting us know God desires to do great things *in and through us*. He not only wants to give us the power to change our own lives, but also to positively influence the lives of those around us. We have the power to do that through the Holy Spirit. The power that created the universe is dwelling within you!

Many of us have a static self-image. We simply believe, "This is who I am; I am unable to change." But as we grab hold of the truth that we have the power of the Spirit within us, we can begin to build a dynamic self-image. A dynamic self-image asks, "Who am I in Christ?" I need to begin dwelling on that question every day, developing a hunger to discover what Christ can do with my life when He is in charge. One thing I do know: He is able to do immeasurably more than all I could ask or think. There is a potential within me that I may have yet to tap into. God desires to transform me as I yield my life to His care and allow Him to fill me with His Holy Spirit.

TRUST AND PATIENCE

To allow God to work in my life, I need two important qualities – trust and patience. Trust comes first. I must trust God if I am going to allow His truth to penetrate my defenses. Any belief can be changed, but the defenses are protecting my beliefs. I have to feel loved enough and safe enough to lower those defenses if I am going to change and grow. If I do not trust God and the life-changing power of the Bible, that truth will not change my heart.

But trust is not easy. Growing up in this fallen world, we discover that people are not very trustworthy. They let us down, lie, manipulate, deceive, etc. Negative experiences can cause us to become very distrusting. After all, it's a dog-eat-dog world out there, and we must protect ourselves. It is very easy to believe that God is in this same category because we will subconsciously feel that God is much like the people we have known.

149

Brain Washed

Worse yet, Satan is always seeking to get us to mistrust God. That is how he tricked Adam and Eve into disobeying God. Before Satan came into the picture, Adam and Eve trusted God completely. But Satan called God a liar and planted a seed of doubt in their mind which began to grow. Satan is still deceiving mankind in this same way. I need to trust God and stop believing Satan's lies when he tells me God is against me rather than for me. Yes, I may experience some awful circumstances in this fallen world, but God does not cause them. These negative, painful experiences are a consequence of living in a sinful, fallen world.

God is not like fallen human beings. I cannot stress that enough. We must get to know God through a healthy, mature understanding of the Scriptures. He is for us, not against us. He loves us more than anyone else ever will or ever could. He values us as His children and will never leave us nor forsake us. We must come to trust God if He is going to be able to change our hearts.

Christian music is another good way to enable God's truth to penetrate the subconscious in order to deepen our trust in God. Music is a safe medium that brings enjoyment and relaxation. Music can help lower our defenses and allow messages, which might otherwise be blocked, to penetrate the subconscious. The value of Christian music is the truth contained in the words of the song, whether it is hymns, choruses, contemporary, country gospel, Christian rock, etc. John Wesley, an eighteenth century theologian and evangelist, took the pub music of his day and put Christian lyrics to it because he wanted to reach those outside the church. The religious people of his day thought it was scandalous. But those same songs became the hymns of the twentieth-century church. Today, everyone can find Christian music that fits their musical tastes. Not only does music help penetrate the defenses, but we will listen to the same songs repeatedly. If the truth of God's Word is contained in those lyrics, subconscious beliefs will change due to the repetition.

But it does take time to change; it will not happen overnight. We discovered that principle in the model for the mind. One of the reasons I ran from God's call as a senior in high school was that I thought, *"I cannot do that. I will surely fail if I try."* But when I stopped running and yielded to His call, I knew I had to *trust* that if He was calling me to do this, He would also equip me. I had to trust Him to work in my life because there were a lot of changes needed. And since the changes would come slowly, I needed *patience*.

Fortunately, I understood that the changes would not come rapidly, and I also realized that I was going to have to cooperate with God. God and I were now a team working together. With that in mind, I shared with my pastor and youth leader the call I felt God had placed in my life and asked them to begin mentoring me. I decided that if they asked me to do something, I would view it as God asking me and not say, "No!" (which was my go-to word before this time).

A few months later, when the youth leader asked me to teach at the next youth meeting, I said, "Yes." Then I went home and prayed and studied like crazy. I am sure it was not the best teaching they ever had, but it definitely went better than I feared. I was being stretched and moving out of my comfort zone. It was not the most pleasant experience, but the resulting growth was worth it.

All through college, I continued to trust the Lord and allowed Him to stretch me. God, in His mercy, took His time so that I could change gradually. As I finished college, I realized how patient God had been with me, but I did not see it that way at first. During my college years, I noticed that God would often focus on one key area of growth at a time. I would see that focus in my classes, in books I was reading, in talking with other students, etc. It would seem to last about six months, and then God would move on to another area of growth. When I first started noticing this pattern, I thought, *"God must be so impatient with me. It takes about six months to get one little concept into my thick brain!"* You can see my negative self-image was still quite active.

Toward the end of my senior year, I realized that God did not simply want head knowledge. He could give me that in one week. Instead, He wanted the change to happen at a deeper level, in my heart, and that is what took time. Rather than being impatient, God was eternally patient with me and wanted me to be more patient with myself. I began to relax and let God work at His pace. He knew me a lot better than I knew myself. Trust and patience were working together in sync as I trusted God to work in my life and then patiently cooperated with Him.

While in college, I attended one of Bill Gothard's seminars entitled, "Basic Life Principles." This was a popular 25-hour workshop, attended by hundreds of thousands in venues all over the world. He covered a variety of life-changing biblical principles. I learned a great deal in those 25 hours, but I especially liked the message which came in the last hour. After the last break, we were all asked to reach into our materials packet and pull out a small lapel button. On it was written these letters: PBPGINFWMY. Bill Gothard then said, "You are probably wondering what this strange jumble of letters means. Here is the answer: PLEASE BE PATIENT, GOD IS NOT FINISHED WITH ME YET." He continued, "You have learned a lot of principles in this seminar and are excited to go from here to try them out. But you must realize, just because you have learned the principles, does not mean that you are going to instantly have your lives changed. You must take these truths and slowly allow them to be integrated into your life. You must let God bring them to memory, time and time again. You must practice these principles and realize you will fail as much as you succeed. But do not give up. God is not finished with you yet, and if you keep working at it, these principles will become a part of your life and bring about wonderful changes. Do not expect to change overnight. You must be patient with yourselves."

The Apostle Paul said basically the same thing in Philippians 1:6, *"Being confident of this, that he who began a good work in you will carry it on to completion until the day of Christ Jesus."* God will never give up on you; don't give up on yourself.

I will now say the same thing to you concerning this book. You have learned some life-changing principles, but it is going to take time to get them into your subconscious. You may be all excited and really want your life to change, but unfortunately, it is not going to happen all at once. If you get impatient, you will be like the person who excitedly heads into the New Year with all his resolutions in hand, only to give up two weeks later saying, "I guess I can't change. I might as well quit trying."

But you can change, and you will change, but you must be patient. You may need to read this book again about every six months to gauge what changes have been happening in your life. I have been working with these principles for more than thirty years and still find new insights as I experience more of life. As subconscious beliefs change, thinking, behaviors, reactions, and feelings change as well. Many times, I do not notice the change until I look back.

Trusting God and understanding the true nature of His Fatherhood is the best way to let Him parent you. You didn't have a chance to choose your parents, who may have been quite dysfunctional, but you do get a chance to choose another parent. God the Father is better than anyone else's parent in the whole world. He desires to take over and help you grow into a healthy adult. How great is that! And learning to be patient with yourself in the process is another way to be your own best friend. With God's help, you can begin living life to its fullest.

PAUL'S MESSAGE TO THE CHURCH IN ROME

When I first started putting these principles together into a workshop in the mid-nineties, I thought I was creating something that was quite unique. I especially liked the ego vs. esteem needs, which I felt explained why we can develop an unhealthy self-love. Also, learning how to "hear" God communicating His love was something I had never come across in any of my studies.

But then as I was studying Romans 7 & 8, I realized that the Apostle Paul had taught all of these principles two thousand years ago. He beautifully shared how God can meet all five of the esteem needs. Now I will admit, he shared them in a different order, but they are all there. In fact, the greatest esteem need, the need to be loved unconditionally, which I dealt with first, he left for last. Perhaps that was the better literary technique – save the best for last as the climax of the story. As the writer of Ecclesiastes said, *"There is nothing new under the sun"* (Ecclesiastes 1:9). We do not discover new truths, we simply rediscover the truth. Each of us needs to rediscover God's truths.

In Romans 7, the Apostle Paul was sharing his story with the church in Rome, similar to what I was doing at the beginning of this book. He was being brutally honest, which I would guess was not easy. (I know it was not easy to reveal my past to you.) As a Pharisee, he had sought to hide his sin most of his life. On the outside, he had looked very righteous, but here he shares what was really happening on the inside.

[14] We know that the law is spiritual; but I am unspiritual, sold as a slave to sin. [15] I do not understand what I do. For what I want to do I do not do, but what I hate I do. [16] And if I do what I do not want to do, I agree that the law is good. [17] As it is, it is no longer I myself who do it, but it is sin living in

me. ¹⁸

me. ¹⁸ For I know that good itself does not dwell in me, that is, in my sinful nature. For I have the desire to do what is good, but I cannot carry it out. ¹⁹ For I do not do the good I want to do, but the evil I do not want to do—this I keep on doing. ²⁰ Now if I do what I do not want to do, it is no longer I who do it, but it is sin living in me that does it.

²¹ So I find this law at work: Although I want to do good, evil is right there with me. ²² For in my inner being I delight in God's law; ²³ but I see another law at work in me, waging war against the law of my mind and making me a prisoner of the law of sin at work within me. ²⁴ What a wretched man I am! Who will rescue me from this body that is subject to death? (Romans 7:14-24).

Did you notice how he kept repeating himself to get his point across? Many people relate to this story. The good things we want to do, we do not do, and the bad things we do not want to do, we do. What is driving this dysfunctional behavior? We know God's law is good, but it is so hard to keep His commands.

Paul realized that sin was an evil force within him. He felt wretched and was describing quite effectively the dysfunctional behavior driven by unhealthy subconscious beliefs. He wondered, *"Who can rescue me from this body that is subject to death?"* He shared the answer in the very next verse:

Thanks be to God, who delivers me through Jesus Christ our Lord! (Romans 7:25).

On the road to Damascus that fateful day when he met Jesus Christ, a change started happening in his heart. But it was not a change that happened quickly. It was slow and steady. He realized that even though he had studied under an excellent Jewish Rabbi, he did not really know God at all. He began seeing God differently now that he had met Jesus Christ. He spent three years in the wilderness focusing on the teachings of Christ, getting to know Christ better, and building an intimate relationship with Christ, his new brother and best friend. I assume he knew that Jesus had spent three years mentoring his disciples and figured he needed at least that long himself before he could begin effectively communicating these wonderful truths to others. He then returned to Antioch and began to help pastor the growing church in that area. It was over a decade later when he began his missionary work, traveling throughout Asia Minor preaching the Gospel, starting new churches, and writing letters to various churches. Letters that ended up filling half of our New Testament.

The growth that changed his life so drastically centered on getting some key truths about God into his heart. As Paul continued his story in Romans 8, he shared the truths that had made those wonderful changes in his life.

ROMANS 8:1-4

[1] Therefore, there is now no condemnation for those who are in Christ Jesus, [2] because through Christ Jesus the law of the Spirit who gives life has set you free from the law of sin and death. [3] For what the law was powerless to do because it was weakened by the flesh, God did by sending his own Son in the likeness of sinful flesh to be a sin offering. And so he condemned sin in the flesh, [4] in order that the righteous requirement of the law might be fully met in us, who do not live according to the flesh but according to the Spirit.

"There is no condemnation for those who are in Christ Jesus." What does no condemnation imply? Unconditional acceptance and forgiveness. In Christ, he discovered acceptance and forgiveness in its purest form. Much different from anything he had ever known as a Pharisee. God was meeting esteem need number three.

ROMANS 8:15-17

¹⁵ The Spirit you received does not make you slaves, so that you live in fear again; rather, the Spirit you received brought about your adoption to sonship. And by him we cry, "Abba, Father." ¹⁶ The Spirit himself testifies with our spirit that we are God's children. ¹⁷ Now if we are children, then we are heirs— heirs of God and co-heirs with Christ, if indeed we share in his sufferings in order that we may also share in his glory.

What is Paul sharing here? He had learned the truth of infinite worth and value through being God's son. He had been fully adopted into God's family. He could call God *Abba.* That was the word that little children called their Father. *Daddy* would be a perfect translation into English. Two simple syllables. I have a feeling that a famous Jewish father listened to the first babble that came from his child's lips and proudly said, "That's me!" There are no two syllables easier to say for a baby than *Abba.* Jewish religious leaders of that day would never dare call God *Abba.* God was too holy and great to be referred to by such an intimate term.

Paul discovered he could call his Heavenly Father *Abba.* He was God's son and co-heir with his brother, Jesus Christ. Everything that belonged to Jesus through sonship was also his. He felt so valued. He was a child of God! God was meeting esteem need number two.

It is vital to understand that, as our Father, He is not going to give us everything we want. That would spoil us. He is also going to allow us to go through some hard times because that is how we grow and develop coping skills. He is a wise Heavenly Father, and everything He allows to happen in our lives is ultimately for our good, even though we may not understand that at the time it is happening.

ROMANS 8:26-28

26 In the same way, the Spirit helps us in our weakness. We do not know what we ought to pray for, but the Spirit himself intercedes for us through wordless groans. 27 And he who searches our hearts knows the mind of the Spirit, because the Spirit intercedes for God's people in accordance with the will of God. 28 And we know that in all things God works for the good of those who love him, who have been called according to his purpose.

Here we see the power of the Holy Spirit. It is alright to admit that we have weaknesses. The Spirit comes to help us with those weaknesses, even to help us pray. He intercedes for us and helps us overcome sin.

God is working for our good through everything we experience. What a promise. That means He helps us grow through our circumstances. We do not have to fear failure. Even when we mess up, God helps us grow through the failure and become better people. We can take risks and accept new challenges. Through the power of His Spirit, we become more confident. We can make wise choices that enable us to rise above our circumstances rather than letting our circumstances overcome us. We receive the power to change and grow. God can meet esteem need number five.

ROMANS 8:29-30

[29] For those God foreknew he also predestined to be conformed to the image of his Son, that he might be the firstborn among many brothers and sisters. [30] And those he predestined, he also called; those he called, he also justified; those he justified, he also glorified.

Paul had discovered that true attractiveness involved being conformed to the image of Christ. He wanted his life to emulate the life that Christ lived. Paul communicated this so beautifully in Galatians 2:20, *"I have been crucified with Christ and I no longer live, but Christ lives in me. The life I now live in the body, I live by faith in the Son of God, who loved me and gave himself for me."* God meets esteem need number four.

ROMANS 8:31-39

[31] What, then, shall we say in response to these things? If God is for us, who can be against us? [32] He who did not spare his own Son, but gave him up for us all—how will he not also, along with him, graciously give us all things? [33] Who will bring any charge against those whom God has chosen? It is God who justifies. [34] Who then is the one who condemns? No one. Christ Jesus who died—more than that, who was raised to life—is at the right hand of God and is also interceding for us. [35] Who shall separate us from the love of Christ? Shall trouble or hardship or persecution or famine or nakedness or danger or sword? [36] As it is written:

*"For your sake we face death all day long;
we are considered as sheep to be slaughtered."*

> *[37] No, in all these things we are more than conquerors through him who loved us. [38] For I am convinced that neither death nor life, neither angels nor demons, neither the present nor the future, nor any powers, [39] neither height nor depth, nor anything else in all creation, will be able to separate us from the love of God that is in Christ Jesus our Lord.*

Paul saves the best for last. The need to be loved unconditionally is the greatest esteem need, which every human being desperately seeks. What a powerful message is communicated through these verses. It was this *agape* love that transformed Paul from the legalistic, judgmental Pharisee into the compassionate, loving, deeply caring Christian missionary. Read these words out loud to yourself. What an impact they have. If you personalize these verses and get them into your heart, they can revolutionize your life. **Nothing, absolutely nothing, can separate you from the love of God that is in Jesus Christ our Lord**.

IN CONCLUSION

The best advice I can give you as you finish this book is simply to be patient with yourself and persevere. That means never give up. Keep working these truths into your subconscious. The stronger the negative beliefs, the longer it may take to enable the belief to become healthy, but if you keep at it, it will happen. Any belief can be changed.

It may be wise to make a list of goals. Select the areas you desire to change in your life and then prioritize them. Work on one or two goals at a time because this is your best chance of successfully bringing about change. To the best of your ability, allow God to help you decide which goals to pursue because He knows you better than you know yourself. Let the Holy Spirit strengthen you from within. You are not alone. Never forget that the Holy Spirit is there to help you. You can also rely on trusted friends to help keep you accountable and encourage you along the way.

As you work consistently on your goal, whether it involves changing a behavior or a conscious thought, it will eventually change your subconscious belief. That is when it gets really exciting. You will not have to work on it as much because the subconscious will take over. You will notice a change has happened in your life. That which you were working on is now a part of *who you are*. You realize you are behaving, thinking, reacting, and feeling differently. At that point, you are ready to focus on another goal or two. Remember, this will take months – not days – for only a couple of changes to be made. But never give up. This is a marathon, not a sprint. Slow and steady trumps fast and erratic every time. God is very patient, and if you allow Him, He will guide you through the process of transforming your life into the image of Christ.

Let this be your daily prayer: "Father, I have the rest of my life, let's see what we can make of it together. I am in Your loving hands."

Who am I in Christ? I am excited to find out!

CHAPTER 12

THE 30 MINUTE 30 DAY CHALLENGE

You may have heard the saying, "Anything I do thirty days in a row is well on its way to being a life-long pattern." Similar catchphrases are common. With our new understanding of the subconscious mind, this quote makes a lot of sense. Let's take everything we have learned and try to apply it to our everyday life.

One of the most important habits you can have is a daily devotional time. It is the few minutes of every day spent reading the Bible and conversing with God in prayer. I have often wondered, *what if I had not had a daily devotional time during my freshman year of college.* It was that special time each morning where God was able to communicate His love in an intimate way. If I had not had that time with God, the truth of God's unconditional love may never have fully penetrated my subconscious.

God loves for us to spend quality time with Him. Think of it as a date. Having regular dates with your spouse keeps the intimacy of your relationship strong. The same is true with our relationship with God.   In Revelation 19:7, the church is defined as the bride of Christ: *"Let us rejoice and be glad and give him glory! For the wedding of the Lamb (Jesus) has come, and his bride has made herself ready."* God desires to have an intimate daily relationship with us.

If you already have a regular devotional time, you know what I am talking about.   But after years of counseling, I have found that many people have never thought about spending time with God on a daily basis.   Again, think of marriage.   If you and your spouse spent one or two quality hours a week together, but then went to separate homes, what kind of marriage would you have? The answer is obvious. Depth in a relationship comes through dwelling together.   Why do we think our relationship with God is any different? If you desire for God to bring about positive changes in your life, you need to spend time with Him.

But there is another important aspect to the devotional time as well. I may have developed a good *habit* of spending time with God, but after a while, the habit can become a ritual and no longer be intimate. We have to work to make the devotional time a good habit while at the same time working to keep it fresh and vibrant. If you can build that type of intimacy with God, you will be amazed at the changes God can make in your life.

To help get you started on that journey, I am giving you a challenge for the next thirty days. Set aside thirty minutes each day for God. Try to pick a specific time of the day because consistency helps in building a good habit. I personally like the morning, but if you are not a morning person, that may not be a good time for you.   Select a time that best fits your schedule.

You may be thinking: *"I just don't have the time."* But ponder this for a moment; I am only asking for two percent of your day; you can do this! At first, you will have to make the time, but once it is a fully ingrained habit, you will always have the time and feel uncomfortable when, on those rare occasions, you have to miss that special time for some reason.

Begin by spending some time reading the Bible. For these first thirty days, I am giving you Bible passages which focus on the five esteem needs. After that, you may want to look for one of the thousands of devotional books on the market today. Also, there are good Bibles and devotionals that can be found on the internet. YouVersion has a wonderful free Bible app for smartphones and other devices which contains a variety of different translations as well as hundreds of Bible studies and devotionals (www.youversion.com/products).

Next, spend time conversing with God. Start by thanking Him for His love, compassion, and forgiveness. Then, thank Him for anything else that comes to mind. Having a positive focus is a wonderful way to begin. This is called praise and worship. Your subconscious will experience you verbalizing these positive affirmations about God. The daily repetition of thanksgiving and praise helps your heart accept these truths.

After spending time thanking God, share your needs and the needs of others with Him. It is good to pray specifically, then you can easily see when God answers those prayers. I would encourage you to keep a journal with a column for prayer requests and a column to write down answers to prayers.

Finally, allow God to speak to you. Prayer is a conversation with God. Remember to personalize verses and allow God to communicate those truths deep into your heart on a daily basis. As you grow accustomed to hearing God speak to you through His word, it will become natural to listen and hear God encouraging you daily.

Plan on spending thrity days on the rest of this chapter. Each day you will have a passage in the Bible to read. Look up the verses and focus on the words. This is God's love letter to you.

When my wife and I began dating over forty years ago, we lived five hundred miles apart. We wrote love letters several times a week. I would read her letter over and over and pretty much have it memorized by the time I received the next letter. We can do the same with God's word.

When you finish reading, ask yourself, "What is God saying to me through these verses?" Then write down your thoughts. A journal is a wonderful way to do this. I have left space in each day's devotional for you to journal right in this book if you so choose. As you think about what God is saying to you, simply talk to God as if He is sitting right next to you because He truly is right there beside you. He promised that He would never leave you nor forsake you (Hebrews 13:5). I have filled in the journal entry for day one as an example. The important thing is to be open and honest with God. That is how He can best speak to you through His word.

To finish your devotional time, I have included a sample verse which is personalized with a blank for you to fill in your name. You can use that to get started, but eventually, simply let God reveal what He wants to share with you and listen. It is through intimate conversation that God can best speak to you. Let Him speak those truths into your heart day after day. That is the best way to help the subconscious come to fully believe the truth of how your Heavenly Father sees you.

Below is a summary of the biblical truths which will be the focus for the next thirty days:

Days 1-6 *Need # 1: The Need to be Loved*
Theme: "The amazing love of God"

Days 7-12 *Need # 2: The Need to be Valued*
Theme: "The Fatherhood of God
and adoption into His family"

Days 13-18 *Need # 3: The Need to be Forgiven*
Theme: "The complete forgiveness which comes
through the sacrificial death of Jesus Christ"

166

Days 19-24 *Need # 4: The Need to be Attractive*
Theme: "Sharing the love, compassion,
and forgiveness of Christ with others"

Days 25-30 *Need # 5: The Need to Grow*
Theme: "Discovering how the power of
the Holy Spirit can change your life"

Thank you for allowing me to share these wonderful truths with you. Enjoy these next thirty days, and may they be the catalyst to a lifetime of growth and change. Allow God to wash your brain through the *"cleansing of His word"* so that you may grow to fully see yourself as God sees you.

THE AMAZING LOVE OF GOD

DAY 1

Read: Romans 8:31-39

Journal: What is God saying to me through these verses?

Dear God, You are for me. What a wonderful truth. I have often felt so insignificant, but the God who created the universe is <u>for</u> puny little me. I guess that means that I am not insignificant? In Your eyes, I was special enough for you to send Jesus to give his life for me. Jesus is interceding for me. I think that means that he is praying for me! He wants me to succeed in life and to become all that You created me to be.

You are telling me that nothing can separate me from Your love. What does that even mean? It is so hard to imagine because I have never felt that secure in this world. But I am going to accept that truth and try to let it sink deep into my heart.

Personalizing a verse: Romans 8:39. Enter your name and allow God to speak these words into your heart.

_____, nothing, absolutely nothing will be able to separate you from My love which comes through Jesus Christ.

DAY 2

Read: I John 4:7-21

Journal: What is God saying to me through these verses?

Personalizing a verse: I John 4:9. Enter your name and allow God to speak these words into your heart.

_____, I showed how great My love is for you by sending My Son to give his life for you so that you can have life through him.

Brain Washed

DAY 3

Read: I Corinthians 13:1-13

Journal: What is God saying to me through these verses?

Personalizing a verse: I Corinthians 13:4 & 13. Enter your name and allow God to speak these words into your heart.

_____, My great love for you is patient and kind.
The greatest gift I give you is My love.

DAY 4

Read: Jeremiah 31:1-4

Journal: What is God saying to me through these verses?

Personalizing a verse: Jeremiah 31:3. Enter your name and allow God to speak these words into your heart.

_____, I love you with an everlasting love. I am drawing you to Myself with My unfailing kindness.

171

DAY 5

Read: John 3:1-21

Journal: What is God saying to me through these verses?

Personalizing a verse: John 3:16. Enter your name and allow
God to speak these words into your heart.

_____, I love you so much that I sent My Son into
the world to sacrifice his life for your sin so that you can put
your faith in him, become a part of My family, and live with
Me forever.

DAY 6

Read: Psalm 86:1-17

Journal: What is God saying to me through these verses?

Personalizing a verse: Psalm 86:15. Enter your name and allow God to speak these words into your heart.

_____, I am compassionate and gracious. I am slow to anger and abound in love and faithfulness toward you.

Brain Washed

THE FATHERHOOD OF GOD AND YOUR ADOPTION INTO HIS FAMILY

DAY 7

Read: Matthew 6:25-34

Journal: What is God saying to me through these verses?

Personalizing a verse: Mathew 6:26. Enter your name and allow God to speak these words into your heart.

_____, the birds are valuable to me. I created them and take care of them. But you are my child and I am your Father. You are much more valuable to Me than everything else I have created. You are special!

DAY 8

Read: Romans 8:14-17

Journal: What is God saying to me through these verses?

Personalizing a verse: Romans 8:15 & 17. Enter your name and allow God to speak these words into your heart.

_____, My Spirit lives inside you. I have adopted you into my family through My son, Jesus. Feel free to call me Father, or even Dad. I have made you heir to everything that I have. You are very special to Me.

DAY 9

Read: I John 3:1-10

Journal: What is God saying to me through these verses?

Personalizing a verse: I John 3:1. Enter your name and allow God to speak these words into your heart.

_____, can you see the great love I have poured out upon you. I have called you My child, and that is who you are!

DAY 10

Read: Psalm 68:1-5

Journal: What is God saying to me through these verses?

Personalizing a verse: Psalm 68:5. Enter your name and allow God to speak these words into your heart.

_____, you may not have a father or a mother right now. Perhaps you never knew your father. But always remember – I am your Father. I will watch over you.

DAY 11

Read: John 1:1-14

Journal: What is God saying to me through these verses?

Personalizing a verse: John 1:12. Enter your name and allow God to speak these words into your heart.

_____, when you receive Me into your heart, when you put your faith in Me, you have the privilege of becoming My child. I am your Father!

DAY 12

Read: Galatians 4:1-7

Journal: What is God saying to me through these verses?

Personalizing a verse: Galatians 4:6. Enter your name and allow God to speak these words into your heart.

_____, because you are My adopted child, I have sent My Spirit to live inside your heart, so that you can feel My nearness and call Me Dad. You are very special to Me!

THE COMPLETE FORGIVENESS WHICH COMES THROUGH THE SACRIFICIAL DEATH OF JESUS CHRIST

DAY 13

Read: Psalm 103:1-12

Journal: What is God saying to me through these verses?

Personalizing a verse: Psalm 103:10 & 12. Enter your name and allow God to speak these words into your heart.

_____, My heart is for you not against you. I do not want you to have to pay for your sin. My Son did that for you so that your sin could be removed from you – an infinite distance – as far as the east is from the west.

DAY 14

Read: Acts 3:17-21

Journal: What is God saying to me through these verses?

Personalizing a verse: Acts 3:19. Enter your name and allow God to speak these words into your heart.

_____, I desire for you to be genuinely sorry for your sin and turn to Me so that your sin may be washed away and your life can be refreshed and made new.

181

DAY 15

Read: Ephesians 1:3-10

Journal: What is God saying to me through these verses?

Personalizing a verse: Ephesians 1:7. Enter your name and allow God to speak these words into your heart.

_____, you have been saved through the blood of My Son. I have forgiven all your sins through the riches of My grace.

DAY 16

Read: I John 1:1-10

Journal: What is God saying to me through these verses?

Personalizing a verse: I John 1:9. Enter your name and allow God to speak these words into your heart.

_____, if you confess your sin to Me, I will faithfully and justly forgive all your sin and cleanse you of all unrighteousness.

DAY 17

Read: Isaiah 1:16-20

Journal: What is God saying to me through these verses?

Personalizing a verse: Isaiah 1:18. Enter your name and allow God to speak these words into your heart.

_____, let Me reason with you. Think about it – sin pollutes you and makes you dirty, but I want to wash you clean by getting the sin out of your life so you will be white as snow.

DAY 18

Read: Luke 7:36-50

Journal: What is God saying to me through these verses?

Personalizing a verse: Luke 7:47. Enter your name and allow God to speak these words into your heart.

_____, it is good to realize that you have many sins because when you experience the fullness of My forgiveness, you will love Me even more – just like I love you.

SHARING THE LOVE, COMPASSION, AND FORGIVENESS OF CHRIST WITH OTHERS

DAY 19

Read: I John 3:16-24

Journal: What is God saying to me through these verses?

Personalizing a verse: I John 3:23. Enter your name and allow God to speak these words into your heart.

_____, this is what I want you to do. Put your faith in My Son, Jesus Christ. Then receive the fullness of My love so that you can love others.

DAY 20

Read: John 15:9-17

Journal: What is God saying to me through these verses?

Personalizing a verse: John 15:12-14. Enter your name and allow God to speak these words into your heart.

_____, this is what I want you to do. Love others just like I have loved you. Sacrifice for your friends just as My Son sacrificed His life for you. I consider you My friend when you treat My children well.

DAY 21

Read: Luke 6:27-36

Journal: What is God saying to me through these verses?

Personalizing a verse: Luke 6:35. Enter your name and allow God to speak these words into your heart.

_____, with My love filling you, you can even love those who mistreat you. If you accomplish this, you will be richly rewarded in My Kingdom because others will see My love in you and be drawn to Me.

DAY 22

Read: Romans 12:9-21

Journal: What is God saying to me through these verses?

Personalizing a verse: Romans 12:9-10. Enter your name and allow God to speak these words into your heart.

_____, grow in My love so that your love will be completely sincere, not fake nor manipulating as is so common today. Be devoted to others, honor them and make them feel special, just as you are special to Me.

Brain Washed

DAY 23

Read: Matthew 5:43-48

Journal: What is God saying to me through these verses?

Personalizing a verse: Matthew 5:46-48. Enter your name
and allow God to speak these words into your heart.

_____, let My love so fill you that you are able to
go further than just loving those who love you. Everyone can
do that. Allow My love to help you love the unlovable
person. Then your love will become more like My perfect
love.

DAY 24

Read: Mathew 25:31-46

Journal: What is God saying to me through these verses?

Personalizing a verse: Matthew 25:40. Enter your name and allow God to speak these words into your heart.

_____, when you help one of My children in any way, I feel like you have done that same thing to Me, and I feel so proud of you.

DISCOVERING HOW THE POWER OF THE HOLY SPIRIT CAN CHANGE YOUR LIFE

DAY 25

Read: Romans 8:1-11

Journal: What is God saying to me through these verses?

Personalizing a verse: Romans 8:11. Enter your name and allow God to speak these words into your heart.

_____, My Spirit, Who raised Jesus from the dead, is living inside of you. He will also raise you up, giving you new life, empowering you to change and grow to become more like My Son.

DAY 26

Read: I Corinthians 12:12-31

Journal: What is God saying to me through these verses?

Personalizing a verse: I Corinthians 12:27. Enter your name and allow God to speak these words into your heart.

_____, you are a part of My body. Do you understand what that means? You have a special part to play in this world, and My Spirit will empower you to do your part and to do it well. I will help you change and grow and become more like Me.

DAY 27

Read: Ephesians 5:8-20

Journal: What is God saying to me through these verses?

Personalizing a verse: Ephesians 5:18. Enter your name and allow God to speak these words into your heart.

_____, in the same way drunk people are inspired to boldly do foolish things, My Spirit can inspire you to boldly do great things for My Kingdom. Be filled with My Spirit.

DAY 28

Read: Genesis 1:1-31

Journal: What is God saying to me through these verses?

Personalizing a verse: Genesis 1:1-2. Enter your name and allow God to speak these words into your heart.

_____, in the beginning, My Spirit created the heavens and the earth. Now, don't you think that same Spirit, living inside of you, can recreate you into something amazing?

DAY 29

Read: Matthew 14:13-21

Journal: What is God saying to me through these verses?

Personalizing a verse: Matthew 14:19-21. Enter your name and allow God to speak these words into your heart.

_____, My Son fed over five thousand people with five loaves and two fish in His hands. What do you think He can do with you if you place yourself in His hands? Watch Him multiply your usefulness.

DAY 30

Read: Galatians 5:13-26

Journal: What is God saying to me through these verses?

Personalizing a verse: Galatians 5:22-23. Enter your name and allow God to speak these words into your heart.

_____, My Spirit can empower you to be loving, joyful, peaceful, patient, kind, good, faithful, gentle, and self-controlled. When these qualities are filling your life, you are doing all I want you to do. Keep growing in My Spirit and have a great life.

DEAR READER,

Thank you for taking the time to allow me to share this book with you. If someone had told me forty-five years ago that I was going to write a book someday, I would have laughed and replied, "In your dreams."

But over the past four decades, God has transformed my life in many wonderful ways, and I wanted to share some of the truths that changed my life in hopes that the same may happen for you as well.

I remind you that the key to change is the subconscious. If your subconscious firmly believes the truth of God's wonderful love, and you begin to see yourself as God sees you, your deepest esteem needs will be met. Your life will feel whole.

But unfortunately that takes time, so I remind you to be patient. You may want to pick up this book again a year from now and read it again. As your beliefs change, your perspectives change as well. You might find yourself grasping these concepts even more fully after you have lived with them for a while. I still gain insight as I continue to apply these principles in my life.

If this book has been helpful for you, I would love to hear from you. It will bless me to know how the book has touched your life. You can send a message or a review of this book by using the *contact form* at HopeAliveCounseling.com.

May God richly bless you, and may He succeed in washing your brain as He has mine!

David Nofziger

Made in the USA
Monee, IL
04 July 2022

98917797R00121